When Your Ex Won't Pay

NANCY S. PALMER &
ANA TANGEL-RODRIGUEZ

P.O. Box 35007, Colorado Springs, Colorado 80935

Library of Congress Catalog Card Number: 94-38141

ISBN 08910-98798

Some of the anecdotal illustrations in this book are true to life and are included with the permission of the persons involved. All other illustrations are composites of real situations, and any resemblance to people living or dead is coincidental.

This publication is designed to provide accurate and authoritative information in regard to the subject matter covered. It is sold with the understanding that the author and the publisher are not engaged in rendering legal, accounting, or other professional service. If legal advice or other expert assistance is required, the services of a competent professional person should be sought. *From a Declaration of Principles jointly adopted by a Committee of the American Bar Association and a Committee of Publishers.*

Palmer, Nancy S.
    When your ex won't pay : getting your kids the financial support they
deserve / Nancy S. Palmer and Ana Tangel-Rodriguez.
        p.   cm.
    ISBN 0-89109-879-8
    1. Child support—United States. 2. Child support—Law and legislation—
United States.   I. Tangel-Rodriguez, Ana.   II. Title.
HV741.P337   1994
362.7'1—dc20   94-38141
                                                                    CIP

Printed in the United States of America

1 2 3 4 5 6 7 8 9 10 11 12 13 14 15 16 17 18 10 20 / 00 99 98 97 96 95

▼ ▼

Contents

My stepfather, Larry Campbell, now deceased,
provided emotional and financial support to me and my sisters
without any legal obligation and with selfless love.
Similarly, my husband Bill has provided
to my son Brent the same love and support.
To these good men I dedicate this book
with love, admiration, and gratitude.
I am also appreciative that my ex-husband
has taken his support obligation seriously.

—Nancy S. Palmer

✦ ✦ ✦

To my children, Ani and Michael,
who through their wisdom have taught me
to have understanding of others,
to recognize my priorities in life,
and to appreciate what a special gift children are.

—Ana Tangel-Rodriguez

CHAPTER ONE

The Way It Is

JOANNA HAD PUT UP with a lot. But the time finally came when she decided that enough was enough, and she filed for divorce. Tom didn't fight it. He simply packed his things into their blue Chevy station wagon, left northern California, and headed for Texas. He didn't even bother to say goodbye.

Although Joanna was left alone with three young children, a pile of bills, a crummy job, and no car, she refused to give in to defeat. "We'll make it somehow," she told her children. "We are all together, and we'll be okay."

At the final divorce hearing, when the judge awarded her $350 a month child support, Joanna breathed a sigh of relief. "Thank goodness that's over," she told her friends. "Now I can begin to put my life back together."

Unfortunately, it was far from over.

For three months, Joanna heard nothing from Tom. Then came a money order for $150, then nothing more. Desperate, she borrowed money from her parents. "Just enough to buy an old clunker of a car," she told them. "Just something to get me to work and back home again. I've got to keep my job so I can support the kids!"

When her parents suggested she put pressure on Tom to pay up on his child support, Joanna said, "Forget him! The kids and I will make it on our own."

Soon after, her seven-year-old son had to quit Cub Scouts. "With the dues and the uniform and everything we have to buy, it's just too expensive," she explained. She also signed the boy up for subsidized lunches at school. "But don't tell Grandma and Grandpa," Joanna warned him. She knew what they would say if they found out that she was barely scraping by from paycheck to paycheck.

Two months later, Joanna got a phone call from the bank that had financed her and Tom's station wagon. They hadn't received any payments for months, they informed her, and if they didn't get one within ten days, her credit would be ruined.

"What?" Joanna exclaimed. "You can't do that! I haven't even seen that car since Tom left California!"

But they *could* do it because Joanna's name was on the loan. So she got a part-time job where she could work weekends, and she started making payments of $200 a month on a car she would never see again. "I have no choice," she cried to her best friend. "It's the only way I can protect my credit."

And still no child-support money from Tom. When Joanna could no longer hide her financial struggle from her parents, they insisted that she call her state caseworker. "When are those child-support payments going to start?" she asked. "I need the money for rent and food and shoes for the kids. And I need it now!"

An order was placed with the Texas child-support agency to deduct the $350 a month from Tom's paycheck and send it to Joanna, but her caseworker warned her that because of the backlog it would take months before Texas even got the order, and then there was no assurance the company he worked for would cooperate.

"Get a lawyer," Joanna's caseworker suggested.

A lawyer? How? Joanna could barely afford to buy food for her little ones. "Maybe in a few months," Joanna said. "I filed my income tax return, and I'll be getting a $750 refund."

Last week Joanna got a letter from the IRS. Tom had made an error on the income tax form he had filed for the two of them three years before and they owed $500. Because Joanna had filed a return for the current year and Tom had not, the IRS was going to deduct the $500 from the $750 refund she was counting on.

"My kids will just have to get used to being poor," Joanna told her parents. "This is how it is, and it's not going to change. There's nothing more I can do."

✦ ✦ ✦

We wish we could say Joanna's case was unusual. But the unfortunate fact is that all across the United States, children like Joanna's are being cheated and shortchanged by parents who refuse to pay for their support.

Failure to pay child support is the largest single crime in the United States. Each year thousands of people file for child support, but less than half of those who are awarded support payments ever receive them. Twenty-five to 30 percent never even get their first payment.

The number of children and custodial parents (usually mothers) who suffer at the hands of deadbeat noncustodial parents (usually fathers) is nothing less than a national disgrace. In no other area of financial responsibility do we tolerate such an appalling performance record. **(Because most custodial parents are mothers and most parents who owe child support are fathers, we will refer to them this way throughout the book. Please understand that this in no way minimizes the importance of custodial fathers or the responsibility of noncustodial mothers who are under court order to pay child support.)**

The numbers of parents and children who could potentially be affected by this irresponsibility is staggering. With almost half of all marriages in this country ending in divorce and with one out of four babies born out of wedlock, approximately half of all children born in the United States today can be expected to spend some time in a single-parent household.

These statistics affect everyone in the U.S. Because of the widespread failure of parents to pay for their children's support, there has been an explosion in the number of welfare recipients. The result is that children have now surpassed the elderly as the single poorest group in the country. Today one in five American children—a total of 14.3 million—lives in poverty.

"I get child support," says one mother of two adolescents, "but every year the gap between what the kids need and what the support money can pay for grows larger and larger. Even working two jobs, I can't keep up with the costs."

This is a common complaint. Even when child support is paid, the payments often fail to keep pace with the rising cost of living and the cost of raising a child. Many times, those payments also fail to reflect the growing income of the absent parent.

This country's system of child support is in trouble, there is no question about that. Almost everyone who is at all knowledgeable about the subject agrees that:

▼ Children are not getting the support money they are owed.

▼ Caseworkers are so overwhelmed that parents seeking help in some areas are faced with day-long busy signals when they telephone and seemingly endless waits when they finally get an appointment.

▼ Paternity identification rates are discouragingly low. Less than one-third of the one million children born out of wedlock every year have their fathers (and rightful supporters) identified.

▼ Child-support guidelines vary widely from state to state. In Connecticut, for instance, two children whose mother earns $1,000 a month and whose father earns $1,500 get $523 in child support per month. In Minnesota, those same two children get $328. That is a difference of $195 per month.

"But a lot of those low-income fathers simply can't afford to pay," many people argue. "They don't earn enough money."

Granted, some people at the lower end of the guidelines may truly have difficulty. However, in recent years people who are working in family law have been seeing a troubling trend: There are more and more delinquent parents who can well afford to support their children.

So why don't parents pay child support? There are a number of reasons. Certainly some—a small minority—are unemployed or disabled and truly do not have the money to send. But most have other reasons. For some, it is a question of revenge. ("She left me and took the kids, so she won't get one red cent out of my pocket!") Sometimes it is a dispute over custody or visitation. ("Since she wants the children all to herself, she can just pay all the bills, too.") Some are upset because there is little accountability. ("I pay the money for the kids, and she spends it on herself.") More and more parents don't pay simply because they don't have to. One deadbeat dad said, "Why should I lay out all that money when I can get away without paying? Hey, there are lots of other things I can do with that money."

Whatever the real reason, most nonpaying parents continue to insist, "I can't afford it!" Yet a 1992 study done by the National Commission on Child Support revealed that many of these protesting parents pay more in a year on car payments than they pay in support for their children.

Can't afford it? Paula Roberts, a lawyer with the Center for Law and Social Policy in Washington, doesn't buy that argument. "It's not a lack of resources, it's a lack of will," she insists. "If you bring a child into the world, I don't think you can, or should, ever turn your back on that child and say, 'I can't afford you anymore.'"

Yet even though there is a great deal of room for improvement, we as a country are making progress in the area of child support. In many ways, single custodial parents are better off today than the single parents of a few years ago.

THE WAY IT WAS

"My children are grown now," Beverly said. "But I'll never forget the endless nightmare I faced when they were young."

Beverly's difficulties were not unique. It used to be that child-support guidelines were nonexistent. There was no uniformity. Judge Jones might rule that a father should pay up to 40 percent of his income to support his three children, while Judge Smith might say, "Fifty dollars a month is plenty." Child support was pretty much at the discretion of the presiding judge. The results were often anything but fair and equitable.

"The judge in our case said that he didn't like to legally burden a father," Beverly continued. "There was no talk about what our children needed or how much it would cost to raise them. Even though my husband was a dentist with a thriving practice, he was ordered to pay just $75 a month. Through the years, that amount was never raised."

In chapter 9 we will look at the options a custodial parent has when the other parent won't pay. Those options are not as positive as they should be, but it used to be that there were no options at all. There was no income deduction or wage withholding. And if a parent left the state, there was no continuity or help between states in getting him to pay. If a father left his family in Idaho and went to Kentucky, his ex-wife and kids were simply out of luck.

Back then, few paid much attention to a child's special needs. No one calculated such variables as a parent's earning capacity or commissions or severance pay. There were few arrangements made for medical or life insurance.

"Actually," Beverly added, "I was probably pretty fortunate. At least I got something. There was no guaranteed child support at all when my children were young."

That all changed in 1984 when Congress required every state seeking federal funding to put laws into place that would establish child-support guidelines. At first, these guidelines were only suggestions. But the follow-up Family Support Act of 1988 required that state support guidelines operate as rebuttable presumptions of the correct support amount. This requirement means that the guideline amount is presumed to be correct and must be used unless there are extenuating circumstances. In order to deviate from the guidelines, it should be determined that there is a compelling reason why the guideline amount would be unfair or inappropriate in a specific case.

That's not all. A federal law required child-support assistance for all single parents who were receiving Aid to Families with Dependent Children (AFDC). A subsequent law required that the same services also be made available to custodial parents who are not on welfare. Today, any single parent can go to the local social service office and, for a minimal application fee of no more than $25 in some states, can qualify for help in enforcing her child-support ruling. The service is available to everyone.

So what about Joanna and the legions like her? The bad news is that although new laws have technically made it easier to collect child support, too many women still don't understand how to take advantage of those laws and make the laws work for them.

WE UNDERSTAND WHERE YOU ARE

Day after day, week after week, we see and talk and work with parents who are consumed with the problems of divorce and child support. We find that most parents truly do care about their kids, and neither mother nor father wants to lose touch with them. However, many issues are involved that have to be considered.

How can both parents have a fair and equitable amount of contact with the children? Who should live in the house, or should the divorcing parents sell it? Should there be alimony paid to one parent? Who is going to pay the attorney's fees? And then there is the whole matter of child support—what is fair for everyone? To us, these are everyday questions that we hear over and over, but to the parents who are asking them, they are terribly personal and pressing concerns. "I need help!" is the cry we hear time and time again.

Money questions are especially distressing because many of the people we see are already deeply in debt. "How much is he going to pay for child support?" is the big question of most mothers, while most fathers ask, "How am I ever going to afford to support myself and pay my children's expenses, too?"

Big questions, and not easy to answer from a legal perspective. In a personal injury case, the court is dealing with just one issue: How much is the injury worth? But in child support, the court must consider so many things: the financing for child care, who will carry and pay for health and dental insurance, who will pay the expenses that are not covered, who will handle house repairs, what happens if the house is sold, what activities the child will be able to afford, where the kids will go to school, what about college or vocational school, what about wedding expenses in the child's future, and on and on. Child support is indeed a multifaceted issue.

Both of us are exceedingly concerned about the subject of child support. Between us we have a great deal of firsthand experience with parents who are struggling to provide the best growing-up environment they can for their children. We know about the frustrations and confusions and struggles that come with pursuing an appropriate level of child support. And we are well experienced at stepping back and helping everyone involved to refocus on what is really important—the well-being of the children.

Yet the two of us see the subject from somewhat different perspectives. To help you understand where each of us is coming from, let us tell you a little bit about ourselves.

Ana

"I know all about working through the social services office," Ana says. "I hold the local legal service contract for Orange County, Florida, to serve in that capacity." This work includes setting support payments, enforcing those payments, establishing paternity, handling paternity actions, dealing with non-paying parents who have left the state, modifying support orders, and dealing with parents who are in contempt of court.

While Ana and the attorneys who work with her are able to

offer all these services at virtually no cost, there is a difference to parents between dealing with a government agency and going through a private attorney.

"We can't hold the hands of distraught parents and offer them encouragement and emotional support. We can't answer telephone calls from anxious women who are desperate to have their questions answered. We don't do mediation work in an effort to settle problems amicably and out of court. Our service is by necessity impersonal, and it operates by the book. It is really unfortunate, but we just don't have the time to do any more. With more than 1,000 new cases coming into our office each month—handling sixty hearings a day!—and only my four associates and myself to manage them, it is absolutely impossible to spend much time with any one person."

In fact, Ana is seldom able to so much as see a person until she meets her at the courthouse. "Even though I am not able to have much contact, I often do have an opportunity to sit down with the person to see if we can work the situation out without actually going into the courtroom."

The drawback of a free service is that clients cannot get the personal time and attention they desire. That's hard for some women to understand. "Many come in and demand, 'Why don't you go out there and find that man?' Or they say, 'Why don't you subpoena all of his IRS records and all his business records and have an accountant go over them and see if he's telling the truth about his earnings?'"

Ana has to answer, "Ma'am, I'm terribly sorry, but we just do not have the time or the funds to allow us to do that."

Even though we attorneys can't have a personal relationship with our clients, the Department of Child Support Enforcement (DCSE) does have a large team of caseworkers who investigate each case, interviewing clients and answering questions as best they can. They too are overworked and overburdened, but they make every effort to be accessible.

Despite its drawbacks, for many people this service is the only possible help with child support. And we can offer some real advantages. The service is generally fast. "We are fortunate to usually be able to set our cases for court in just a few weeks," Ana says. And most often the process is simple and straightforward. Also, the DCSE has access to information that private lawyers usually don't from places such as the IRS, unemployment compensation, the Department of Labor, and credit bureaus. And such remedies are available to us as IRS intercepts, unemployment compensation deductions, and having the arrearage placed on a nonpaying parent's credit history.

"When the child support is intertwined with other issues, such as custody or visitation disputes, or property distribution, I sometimes suggest a client call a private lawyer or a mediator," Ana says. "Someone like Nancy."

Nancy

Within her private practice in the area of family and marital mediation, Nancy is especially concerned with issues involving the welfare of children.

"I have been a certified civil and county mediator since 1988 and a family mediator since 1984," says Nancy. "It is my aim to work things out in such a way that big problems never come up. And very often this result can be accomplished. Fully 70 percent of the cases that are mediated in the state of Florida are settled without going to court."

Because Nancy has the luxury of sitting down with the parents involved, talking with them and asking and answering questions, she is able to reach out beyond the basic child-support guidelines laid down by the government, something Ana is seldom able to do. Occasionally, she has the opportunity to come up with truly creative solutions to troublesome cases.

For example, a man had been told by his girlfriend that she was going to have his baby. When he insisted he wanted nothing to do with the child, the woman told him, "All right, just pay me $3,000 for the baby's support and my medical bills, and I will never bother you again." The two signed an agreement between them, and the payment was made. But when the child was fifteen, she came to see Nancy as a lawyer about getting more support for herself.

"We had to fight very hard against the allegation that this matter had already been settled," Nancy recalls. "Only when the court ruled that the ongoing rights of a child couldn't be given away was our action allowed to move forward."

This father happened to be well-off financially and could easily afford to support his daughter. In the end, the girl was awarded a substantial amount that was put into a trust for her. It could be dipped into for the costs of her upbringing, but a significant amount would still be left to finance a college education, something that would not have otherwise been possible.

"This kind of settlement is rare," Nancy emphasizes. "Our overwhelming responsibility is to do what is best for the child, and most psychologists are convinced that what children really need is both parents involved in their lives. With this goal in mind, the courts try hard to encourage both parents to actually parent. Paying is not enough 99 percent of the time."

The luxury of working on a more personal level allows time to consider factors such as each parent's debts, day-care expenses, and so forth.

"I used to be a strong supporter of always keeping both parents in a child's life," Nancy says. "But a certain case made me rethink my position. I was working with a woman whose boyfriend had to come in for blood testing. I happened to see them in the parking lot afterward. Their two-year-old son was strapped into his car seat, and right there in front of him, his parents turned on each other with such hatred and vicious fury that I was really afraid someone would be badly hurt. I honestly did not believe those two parents would ever be able to cooperate in parenting that child.

"Right there in that parking lot I decided that in some instances children actually are better off with one parent than with two. While this is an extreme case, a high degree of constant conflict between parents can cause the emotional death of a child."

While it is true that when we talk about child support

every person's case is different, there is also a great deal that is the same.

THIS BOOK IS FOR YOU

"Since my divorce, I have lost my home and have had to move in with my sister and her family," Sally said. "My kids are upset about having to go to a new school where they don't know anyone, we're way too crowded with my sister's family in their apartment, and I'm terribly worried about what we are going to do for money. So far I'm not getting any child support at all."

Sally needs to see an attorney.

"But there are so many complicated factors in our situation, and I know so little about the process," she said. "It would cost me a fortune in attorney fees just to find out about the guidelines and everything. And I probably couldn't understand them anyway!"

This book was written for people like Sally—and for people like you. When you go into an attorney's office or into a government social services office, you will be in a much stronger negotiating position if you are aware, prepared, and armed with the facts that surround your case. If the attorney doesn't have to take the time to discuss all the basics with you, your bill could be much lower. Whether you meet with a private lawyer or a social services investigator, it will be well worth your time to make yourself knowledgeable about the options you have and the services available to you. You will also find the entire process much less intimidating and confusing. You will walk in to that office feeling far more powerful and much less at the mercy of others.

"I could never understand all that legal mumbo-jumbo," Sally protested. "After all, I only have a high school education."

Good news! It's not all that difficult. In this book we are going to help you understand what the law does and does not offer you, what the state and federal guidelines are, and just what you can and cannot realistically expect from a child-support judgment. In chapter 4 we will walk you through the entire process. Then we will address some specific concerns you likely share with many other single parents: the emotional impact of all this, the special concerns of women seeking child support from fathers who were never their husbands, and how to fit in with the needs and concerns of your child's father's other family and perhaps your new family.

"Well, I have a friend who has a child-support order, but her husband won't pay," Sally continued. "What if that happens to me? What will I do then?"

Good question, and one many custodial parents have to confront. That's why we have dedicated an entire chapter to enforcing the order.

"But I just can't help feeling that maybe I'm not being fair, or that maybe in the end getting the child support is not worth the battle," Sally confided.

With very few exceptions, it certainly is worth it. Supporting one's children is not only fair and equitable, it is the law of the land. And please keep this truth firmly in your mind: By enforcing the law, you are caring for your child. Sure it can be a battle. Sure it sometimes gets so frustrating that you feel like climbing into bed, pulling the blankets over your head, and forgetting the whole thing. But believe us when we tell you, *it is worth the fight.* Your child is worth it.

"My friend's husband didn't pay child support, and she really got back at him," Sally added with a laugh. "She wouldn't let her ex see the kids! When he came to pick them up, she made sure they weren't at home, or at least that there was something better going on so they wouldn't want to go. Sounds like a pretty good idea."

Sometimes you'll hear a parent who has been denied visitation say, "If I can't drive the car, I'm not going to pay for it— same with my kids." This is shortsighted. There are other remedies for contact interferences. Not only is it not in the child's best interest to be kept away from his or her father, it is against the law.

If you are a parent who carries the primary responsibility of your child—even if you are just now starting the divorce process—this book will help you to understand the legal system and to learn how you can go about claiming what lawfully belongs to your child.

The important message for Joanna and Sally, and for you as well, is this: *You can help yourself. You can help your child. And it is your responsibility to do both.*

▼ ▼

CHAPTER TWO

After the Divorce

DIVORCE IS ONE OF the greatest traumas of life. Much more than a single event, it is a process that begins somewhere in the past and continues on years after the divorce is final.

"When I filed for divorce I remember thinking, *At least Michael is out of my life*," Susan said. "I thought I wouldn't have to deal with him anymore. Boy, was I wrong!"

If you are going through a divorce, or if you have just completed the process, you should understand that your relationship with your spouse is not coming to an end if you are parents. It's just changing. You still share your children.

The timing doesn't seem fair, does it? Just when you are feeling especially weak and vulnerable and confused, when your financial resources are quickly dwindling, when you are feeling at your very lowest, that is the time when you are called upon to muster the resources to lay the groundwork for the rest of your child's childhood and adolescent years. You are going to need to pull together all the mature thinking and rational actions you possibly can. What you do now, or what you fail to do, is going to have a tremendous effect on your child's future and on your own future as well.

"But the person I was married to is impossible!" you may be saying. Or perhaps, "All I want now is to have him out of my life!"

We sympathize with your feelings. But what you must understand is that the issue is no longer your relationship with your ex-spouse. What matters now is your child's rights and well-being throughout his or her life until after high school. Given your means and the means of your ex, you have a responsibility to provide the best possible life for that child.

THERE OUGHT TO BE A LAW

"Michael pays support for our three children—if you can call the few dollars I get support," Susan said in disgust. "I mean, it is so unfair. I have a friend who lives across the country who only has two kids, and her ex-husband earns less money than Michael does, yet she gets more support than I do! Aren't there any laws about child support?"

As a matter of fact, there are. Unfortunately, those laws are often so conflicting and confusing that they become a tangled maze, antiquated and terribly hard to struggle through. Even with recent improvements, the child-support system is frustrating.

On the positive side, we will say that most of the laws in the U.S. attempt to strike a balance between rights and responsibility. For instance, in Florida, if a man doesn't provide financial support for the mother of his child, including pre-birth and emotional support, he may well be waiving his right of consent for the adoption of that child. That means that if the child's mother decides to put the baby up for adoption, he no longer has a say in the matter. Some states have very strict abandonment statutes: If a parent pays no child support for a year and if he doesn't contact the child for a year, he loses his rights to that child. The child can be adopted by a stepparent or whoever else might have a legitimate reason to do so.

Yes, Susan, there are laws. They may not go far enough, and they may be frustratingly inconsistent, and they may not always be enforced, but there are laws. And the good news is, *the law is on your side*.

Let's take a look at the laws that are currently in place, beginning with the federal statutes that affect parents throughout the country. Then we will look at the state statutes, where there can be great variations from state to state.

FEDERAL LAWS

In an effort to stem the tide of mothers and children flooding onto the welfare rolls, the federal government has made a real effort to find solutions to the child-support crisis. It has not been easy because child support has traditionally been considered a matter for the individual states to handle. But in 1975, Congress began a series of reforms by enacting Title IV-D of the Social Security Act. (This relates to Ana's department that we told you about in chapter 1.)

Title IV-D accomplished two important things: It created a federal Office of Child Support Enforcement (OCSE); and it required all states to establish child-support offices. Today this program helps locate absent parents, helps establish parentage, sets up and enforces child support, and even helps modify support when a parent's circumstances change. All of these services are available to you, wherever you live and whatever your income.

Nine years after Title IV-D was enacted, Congress added sweeping reforms to the child-support laws. They unanimously passed the Child Support Enforcement Amendments of 1984, then four years later strengthened much of the law with the Family Support Act of 1988, which went into effect in all fifty states by January 1994. Under this act, child-support collections were computerized, a series of time-lines and standards regarding the processing of child-support cases was adopted, and each state was required to establish its own guidelines.

Finally there were some teeth in the law. Now a parent who didn't keep up with his child-support payments could have the support order enforced by such means as having money withheld from his wages or having liens placed on his real and personal property. If he denied he was the child's father, the Family Support Act allowed for help in establishing parentage, even through genetic testing. And now there were provisions to help speed the entire process through the system.

"That's all well and fine if that other parent hangs around," you may be saying. "But what if he leaves the state?"

The lawmakers thought of that, too. Under the Uniform Reciprocal Enforcement of Support Act (URESA), deadbeat parents who have moved to another state will find their court-ordered support enforced in that new state by such methods as having their income or military allotments withheld or having federal and state income tax refunds intercepted and used to pay the support due.

The interstate effort became even more determined in October 1992 when President George Bush signed a law that made crossing state lines to avoid paying child support a federal crime. Now nonpaying parents can be extradited to the state in which the issue was ordered, and criminal charges can be leveled against them in federal court.

It's a great start, and hopefully, still more help is coming. If proposed federal bills are passed, it will become easier to track nonpaying parents across state lines through their professional licenses, their vehicle registrations, and their driver's licenses.

For deadbeat parents who move to another state in an effort to evade their responsibilities, the laws are there. So why is the support collection rate still low? Because, too often, those laws are not aggressively enforced.

STATE LAWS

In addition to the federal laws, each state now has its own specific laws. These laws lay out the way in which each particular state evaluates families and determines what its lawmakers consider a fair and equitable payment for the support of children in that state.

A whole spectrum of state child-support enforcement laws exist to support those guidelines. In Florida, for instance, a delinquent parent who has the good fortune to win the lottery can have those winnings intercepted and applied to his overdue child-support payments. Not too long ago a fellow won $9,000, which happened to be the very amount he owed in back support payments. He quickly headed back to South America—but he went without that money!

Michigan has an especially successful child-support enforcement program known as The Friends of the Court. In effect for over fifty years, many consider it the best in the country.

Many other states are looking into a variety of novel ideas. In Florida, a law went into effect in 1993 that entitles custodial parents and Title IV-D agencies to petition the court to suspend or deny professional licenses to parents who are delinquent in their child-support payments. This concept has been extended to include driver's licenses. California, Maine, Massachusetts, Pennsylvania, and a number of other states have similar provisions. New Jersey, New York, Texas, Wisconsin, and others have similar bills currently awaiting approval.

It certainly sounds promising.

"But suspending professional licenses is a double-edged sword," Nancy warns. "When you take away a person's ability to practice his profession—whether he is a veterinarian or a hairdresser or a dentist or whatever—then how is he going to earn money? And if he can't earn money, how is he ever going to catch up on all those overdue support payments, let alone keep current on his monthly payments?"

In actual practice, suspending licenses is not going to happen often. It is too difficult a process. The intention is that the remedy be one of last resort. But the very fact that it can be done helps to discourage parents from ignoring their court-ordered child support. And it does seem to work. California has a similar provision that went into effect in November 1992. When the California Supreme Court warned that any lawyers who were delinquent in their child-support payments would be suspended, the list of delinquent attorneys dropped from 109 to 14. Florida's supreme court refused to require a specific rule on child support because it reasoned that the general rules on unlawfulness would cure the problem. However, a recent ruling on an attorney complaint suggests a specific rule is needed.

Pennsylvania law allows the names of delinquent parents

to be publicized. In Massachusetts, custodial parents can track down delinquent fathers and mothers through such records as utility bills, employment records, and lists of union employees.

"So what are the laws and regulations in my state?" you may be asking.

We wish we could tell you specifically. But there are so many variations from state to state, and the laws change so frequently, that we cannot possibly list them all here. It isn't hard for you to find out the statutes that apply in your state, however. All you have to do is go to your local public library and look up your state statutes. Most libraries also have special materials to help parents such as yourself as they make their way through divorce and the concerns of securing and enforcing child support. Tell the reference librarian what you are doing and ask for help. You can also contact the Office of Child Support, 4th Floor Aerospace Building, 370 L'enfant Promenade, Washington, DC 20447. The telephone number is (202)401-9373. It keeps up-to-date records on the statutes of all fifty states.

A good place to begin to understand the child-support laws is at the starting point: the state guidelines.

WHAT ARE GUIDELINES?

When lawmakers decided that something had to be done about the multitude of parents who were delinquent in their child-support payments, they determined that the first step to reform would be to establish guidelines that would lay out a formula to determine what basic support should be. The idea was to make child support more consistent and predictable both within a state and from one state to another.

Each state has the same basic aim—to have its guidelines reflect a traditional or appropriate lifestyle for families that fall within similar income levels. For instance, it is neither fair nor acceptable that Peter, James, and John Johnson, whose father earns $35,000 per year, should have to subsist at a far lower standard of living than the majority of other three-child families with a $35,000 annual income, simply because Mr. Johnson no longer lives with his children. Nor is it acceptable that Mr. Johnson would pay $400 in monthly child support when Mr. Williams down the street, who has the same income and similar responsibilities, pays only $250.

That's not to say guidelines have made support payments consistent across the country. They haven't. But they certainly have gone a long way toward making child-support orders more uniform and more predictable. Now that all fifty states have some sort of guidelines in place, when a support case comes before a judge, that judge is presented with a formula that must be followed unless specific factors allow him or her to deviate from the guidelines. It is all predetermined, concrete, and laid out in black and white.

In chapter 3 we will look at state guidelines in more detail. But the important thing at this point is to know that while the establishment of guidelines has been a great help to parents like you, these guidelines are not the final solution to the child-support problem. In fact, they can actually present difficulties of their own. Many attorneys tend to look at a divided family and say, "Well, we have guidelines to cover cases like yours. We'll just stick to them and fill in the blanks on the form."

The problem is that this approach means attorneys are less likely to communicate effectively a client's particular situation to him or her. There are so many ins and outs, exceptions and unique aspects, and further considerations that are appropriate in any particular case, that sticking strictly to the guidelines may be inappropriate.

Here's where you come in. If you don't push to explain your own particular circumstances to your attorney and work to hammer out the exceptions and explore the possibilities of your own unique situation, you can be sure your case will go into court just the way it is. Once there, it may be handled on an impersonal level. It is up to you to make sure your attorney recognizes the guidelines for what they are—merely the basic foundation upon which your case will be built. On the other hand, if there are no special circumstances in your particular case, don't be unrealistic and expect that the guidelines won't apply to you.

Determine to make yourself knowledgeable and become informed. Be prepared to act wisely, responsibly, and with maturity. You owe it to your child.

DIVORCE AFFECTS CHILDREN

Day after day we see the frustration and anger that overwhelm parents who are struggling with the many ramifications of divorce. Our hearts go out to every one of them.

"I was in court the other day, and I saw a little boy sporting a tee-shirt that read: MY DAD IS A JERK," Nancy says. "I longed to search out that child's mother and tell her I understood that she was struggling with an awful lot. But I also wanted to let her know that her 'statement' may well be doing a great deal more harm to her child than the lack of financial support. I can't defend a parent who fails to pay support, but two wrongs don't make a right."

In chapter 5, we will talk about the emotional roller coaster that at one moment allows you to soar with hope that things are finally going to get better, then suddenly crashes you to the depths of despairing certainty that nothing will ever be okay again. But right here we need to remind you that despite your frustration, despite your confusion, despite your bouts of overwhelming hopelessness, it is vital for you to stay in control. Perhaps your ex-spouse *has* acted like a first-class jerk. Perhaps you think it is next to impossible to find anything good to say about him. But it is precisely when your frustration grows that you need to stop, step back, take a couple of deep breaths, and renew your determination to keep all things in perspective. There is a balance between not telling your child lies and forgetting they take their own self-esteem from their biological parents. What attracted you to your ex? Remind your child of those things!

The attitude that will exist between your ex-spouse and your child will depend to a large degree on how you handle yourself during this most challenging of times. Without a doubt, your child will be better off being able to love and care about both her parents and being assured that both parents love and care about her. Many parents don't realize that when they say negative things about their child's other parent, they are in fact hurting that child.

But you may be surprised to learn that *you* will also be better off with your ex involved in your child's life. Studies have shown that a positive relationship between a child's parents generally encourages the noncustodial spouse to keep up with his support payments. It also encourages him to take an active interest in visiting his child and being an important part of the child's life. If you allow your ex and your child to love and care about each other, chances are you will have fewer worries about collecting overdue child-support payments.

As difficult and painful as this time is for you, keep in mind that it is also a time of pain, confusion, fear, and anxiety for your child. Again and again people ask us, "How can I ease my child's hurt in all of this?"

Here is what we tell our clients: The best way to help your child deal with his feelings is to let him see you doing your best to cooperate with his other parent. You can do a great deal to ease your child's pain by reaching beyond your own anger and determining to work together with your ex-spouse, even if it is only for your child's good. This means resisting the temptation to blame him and refraining from arguing and fighting in front of your child. It means never, ever turning on your child and threatening, "If you don't behave, I'll pack your suitcase and send you to live with your father!"

On the positive side, you can reassure your child that the divorce was not her fault. You can encourage her to express such feelings as fear, anger, and hopelessness. You can give her permission to go right on loving both Mom and Dad without taking sides. You can reassure her that whatever happens between you and your ex, she will always be loved and cared for.

Please understand, what is really damaging to a child is one or both of these two things: losing the ongoing relationships with both mother and father, or witnessing continual conflict between her parents. The good news is that serious problems can usually be prevented when parents are willing to rise above their multitude of problems and hurts and to put their child's interest ahead of their own pain and anger.

"But you don't understand," you may be saying. "My ex and I cannot work together. We don't even like each other!"

No matter. Contrary to popular belief, parents can work together even if they don't like each other. Swallow your pride and your resentment, however deserved it may be, and get along for the sake of your child.

FOR THE FUTURE

"The kids in my son's life management class at school are talking about child support and what it means to be required to pay support if you father a child," Nancy says. "I think that school is on the right track. We need to start talking to our kids about responsibility at an early age. Children need to learn from a young age that with rights comes responsibility."

Ana adds, "We're seeing younger and younger parents wrestling with these support issues. It's not uncommon to see thirteen and fourteen-year-olds having babies. Not long ago I talked to a twenty-nine-year-old, never-been-married father of eleven children. He can't understand why so much is taken out of his minimum wage paycheck to help support all those kids. That young man has absolutely no concept of his responsibility to those children."

Recently, the Family Law Section of the American Bar Association instituted a high school curriculum to teach couples how to better communicate when they are in dispute. Programs like this *partners* program will with any luck be adopted nationwide.

The most valuable thing any of us can do for our children is to teach them responsibility, then to model it in the way we take control of the important areas of our lives.

▼ ▼

Just What Is Child Support?

"I DON'T GET ANY child support," Janette said in disgust. "I mean, I get a little money every month from the kids' father, but it isn't enough to really be considered support."

"My eighteen- and twenty-year-olds are in college," Maxine told us. "Both of them live at home where I pay their expenses. So how come they're not getting support any more?"

"When my baby was born, I wanted nothing to do with her father, my ex-boyfriend," Leah recalled. "My parents said I could live with them and they would help with the baby, so I told Robert I didn't want anything from him. Well, things have changed. My parents aren't here any more. Now I wish I had some help from Robert."

Kate said, "My ex-husband says to me, 'Why do you think you should get so much money in child support? The kids don't eat that much, and they can wear only so many clothes!' He has no idea what it costs to raise the children. Just what is child support, anyway?"

That is a good question. Let's look at what child support does involve.

WHAT IS CHILD SUPPORT?

Simply put, child support is money that is paid for the maintenance and benefit of a minor child. And Kate is absolutely

31

right. It takes far more than the cost of food and clothes to raise children. There are health expenses and school expenses such as supplies and field trips. There are sports fees, club dues, and music and dance lessons. There are birthday parties, lunch money, hair cuts, and bikes and skateboards and books and Barbie dolls. When a note comes home from school that says, "Your child needs to bring a gallon of orange juice on Friday for the class party," the price of that orange juice is part of the cost of raising your child.

And what about Leah's decision not to ask for support for her child? That was not a decision for her to make. A parent cannot waive support on behalf of a child. We have mothers who come to see us and say, "I don't want support as long as the father will agree never to see my child." That is not the mother's right. The right to be financially supported by both parents belongs to the child.

We talked in chapter 2 about state guidelines that set a foundation for child-support payments. Let's look at those guidelines more closely to see what they mean to parents.

GUIDELINES FOR CHILD SUPPORT

"How could anyone think I can possibly support four children on the amount of child support I get from my kids' father?" Janette asked. "I can't make money stretch that far."

When she was asked about her contributions to the children's support, she was genuinely shocked. "What?" she exclaimed. "I'm the one who takes care of them. Their father should be the one supporting them."

Janette is not the only woman to be under the mistaken impression that the financial support of children is the responsibility of the parent who isn't taking care of them. Actually, child-support guidelines are based upon income sharing—that is, both parents' incomes are taken into consideration. Depending on your circumstances, you may have support responsibilities too.

The specifics of how the support is calculated—whether

on the gross income or the net income, for instance—are spelled out in the laws of each state. Then, depending on how many children are involved, an attorney needs only to follow a chart to find the amount of money the state has determined necessary to raise a child.

Actually, the process isn't quite as easy as that. Deductions and credits can also be applied. For instance, in many states the cost of child care can be deducted from the base amount. Some states take the cost of health insurance into consideration.

"You need to look over the guidelines worksheet yourself," Ana advises. "Don't just turn it over to your attorney."

The guidelines are not hard to work out. For the most part, it's just a matter of plugging in numbers. Of course, you do have to make sure all the numbers are included and that they are correct.

You say you're not good with numbers? You don't have to be. But you can still figure out the worksheets. If you feel really insecure about your ability, search out a friend who is good with figures and ask him or her to go over the worksheet with you. (To give you an idea of what you will be working with, you will find some examples of guideline worksheets in appendix B, see pages 161-164.)

When you talk with your attorney, he or she will remind you that the court can consider many different things—a child's disabilities, any special needs he might have, exceptional abilities in music or athletics, other children who require support from that parent, and so forth. It's important that you have those extra considerations firmly in mind, because it is awfully easy for an attorney to neglect the extras when filling out the guidelines worksheet. From the attorney's point of view, it takes more time and effort to argue those exceptions. From your point of view, enumerating them can mean extra resources to help meet your child's extra needs.

While federal law requires that each state have child-support guidelines, it does not require any particular set of guidelines. Although they vary from state to state, they tend to be developed around three basic models: the percentage approach to establishing child-support amounts, the income shares model, and the Melson formula. While these approaches are different, all three provide methods for calculating the amount of child support, and all provide for adjustments based on other factors.

Let's look at each of these three models.

THE THREE BASIC MODELS

The Percentage Approach

In this income model, the parent who does not live with the child pays a set percentage of his income in child support. This percentage goes up according to how many children he has. In most states, the percentage remains constant no matter how much the parent earns.

Here are a couple of examples to show you how this approach works: Richard lives in Wisconsin, and Martin lives in Tennessee. If these men each had one child, Richard would pay 17 percent of his income in child support, while Martin would pay 21 percent. If each man had two children, Richard's child support would increase to 25 percent, and Martin's to 32 percent. The amount would continue to increase with each extra child until it topped out at five children. If the two men each had five or more children, Richard would pay 34 percent of his income in child support, while Martin would pay 50 percent.

Some states decrease the percentage assessed as the non-custodial parent's income increases. The reasoning is that the actual amount of money spent on behalf of a child increases as the parent's income increases, although the actual *percentage* of the parent's income that goes to the rearing of that child decreases. Here is an example of what we mean: It may take 25 percent of the income of a father earning minimum wage to support his child. If that father's fortunes should change to where he was earning $50,000 a year, he would likely spend many more dollars on his child, but he wouldn't spend 25 percent ($12,500).

There are some advantages to the percentage model.

Certainly it is simple to apply. And it is easy for parents to figure out exactly where they stand. But one big drawback is that this method doesn't take into consideration how much or how little actual money the *custodial* parent contributes to the child's support. Whether Mom is a surgeon or a waitress or unemployed, Dad's percentage remains the same.

The fifteen states that currently base their child-support guidelines on this approach are: Alaska, Arkansas, California, District of Columbia, Georgia, Illinois, Massachusetts, Minnesota, Mississippi, Nevada, North Dakota, Tennessee, Texas, Wisconsin, and Wyoming.

Income Shares Model

This model combines both the mother's income and the father's income so that the child is able to benefit from both. A chart lists a support figure for varying income levels, then that amount is divided between the two parents based on the amount each parent earns. Both parents also share proportionately in such added expenses as child care, medical insurance, and any medical expenses not covered by insurance.

The idea behind the income shares is that both parents should share in the cost of supporting a child, just as they likely would have if the family had stayed together.

The majority of states have guidelines based on the income shares model.

The Melson Formula

This model for child support was developed by a Delaware judge by the name of Elwood F. Melson, Jr. It has been used throughout Delaware since 1979, although it was last revised in 1990. It is the most comprehensive of the models because it considers a number of factors.

The idea behind the Melson formula is that child support should be based on the estimated cost of raising a child, yet it should also keep back a minimum reserve to allow the parents to support themselves.

This more complicated model involves several steps. The

first step is to calculate the basic amount of support needed. Then, as in the income shares model, this amount is divided between the two parents according to the income of each. Next, a standard of living allowance, based on each parent's remaining income, is applied. Finally, actual child-care expenses are added to the support award for the custodial parent, who will actually be caring for the child.

The unique thing about this formula is that in addition to meeting a child's basic needs, it allows that child to benefit from either parent's higher standard of living. Its drawback is that many consider the formula too complex to be practical.

Besides Delaware, a version of the Melson formula has been enacted in three other states: Hawaii, Montana, and West Virginia.

✦ ✦ ✦

Whichever formula your state uses, accurate income information is the key to ending up with a fair support award.

In 1991, a case went before the Virginia court of appeals in which a judge awarded less than the guideline amount. The trial judge's reasoning was that if he followed the guidelines, it would increase the child support to three times the amount the couple had stated in their separation agreement. The appeals court decided that reason was not good enough to deviate from the guidelines (*Richardson v. Richardson*).

Please understand that guidelines have not made attorneys obsolete. They have merely shifted the focus from proving what the child can get by on to proving what the parent can and should pay. Attorneys still must determine whether the guideline award is appropriate in any specific case. All guidelines list particular factors that can allow a deviation from the guideline amount. We will look at some of these factors later on in this chapter.

"But I don't have a job," Janette said. "How can they consider *my* income when I don't have any?"

All states have the concept of *imputing income*. This means that if the court believes Mom should go out and earn a specific amount of money, or if it determines that Dad should earn more money than his present income, a judge can consider the income that the parents *should be* earning. In Iowa, a college-educated father had been working for fifteen years at a part-time job where he earned minimum wage. Even though he had been under-employed for all those years, long before his child was born, the court ruled that he should pay child support at the level at which he *could* earn money. The court stated it could see no reason why this father should not at least be working full-time (Iowa Dept of Human Services ex rel. *Gonzales v. Gable*, 1991).

When guidelines were first being put into use, lawmakers and attorneys looked at the idea with a good many doubts and suspicions. But several years have passed since guidelines have been in use, and there are now a lot more believers. The guidelines do seem to be working. Support awards are higher and more equitable, and the entire process takes less court time. In addition, more cases are settled and those that are litigated are often narrowed in scope.

Yet the guidelines are only a starting point. Let's look at some of the common factors that can affect the final award.

INSURANCE

"My ex was ordered to pay health insurance premiums for our kids," Kate said. "The other day Brendan, my six-year-old, got hit in the head with a baseball. I rushed him to the emergency room and got the surprise of my life. He had no insurance coverage! His father dropped the kids from his policy and 'forgot' to tell me."

"Unfortunately, this is not an uncommon occurrence," Ana says. "In fact, I have suggested that there be a law requiring insurance companies to notify a custodial parent if medical insurance is dropped."

Medical insurance can be a big problem, more than just the question of who should pay the premium.

"My wife takes the kids to the emergency room for every

little ache and pain, then she presents me with the bills," one dad complained. "I want the kids healthy, but this is ridiculous!"

There are a couple of possibilities for making the cost of health care more fair. One approach would be to divide the cost on a pro-rata basis established on the parents' income. If parents had to share in the uncovered expenses, they would both have an incentive to make wise decisions about the circumstances under which it was appropriate to see a doctor.

Here is another possibility that many people suggest: "I'll pay for the doctor when the child is in my care, and you pay when he's in your care," they say. At first this plan sounds logical, but there are a couple of problems with it. First of all, the primary parent is likely to be around for the majority of the child's accidents and illnesses, which means she is the one who ends up doing most of the paying. Not a very fair arrangement. This approach also opens up a great opportunity for game playing. "I didn't take her to the doctor because I didn't think it was that serious. If you think she needs it, you take her." And, of course, you pay.

So what should you do? That depends. Do you work at a company that offers health insurance? Does your ex-spouse? Which of you has the best policy, both in terms of the deductible and the coverage? Do you both share the cost of the insurance premium? Are you able to agree on the best way to cover uninsured costs? Will your doctors accept direct payment from the insurance company? This method would avoid the problem where the custodial parent pays the doctor directly, the claim is filed through the other's insurer, the insurer pays that parent, and the money never makes it to the paying, custodial parent.

It is best if the two of you can work together to find a way to provide for your child. If that isn't possible, gather the information and bring it to your attorney or mediator. He or she will be better able to assist you if all the facts are presented.

Recently, the federal government enacted legislation to help people like Kate. It allows employees to withhold money not only for support, but also for health-care insurance premiums, through the entry of a Qualified Medical Child Support Order.

SPECIAL NEEDS

One difficult problem child-support guidelines present is a gap between the stated guideline amount and the money actually needed for the support of a specific child. While guideline amounts are based on the average needs of children in general, the needs of a specific child may be very different. An example would be a child with learning disabilities.

"Because I have a master's degree in learning disabilities, I've had a fair number of people come to me to represent them or mediate in these situations," Nancy says. "These families often have such additional expenses as tutoring or private school. Very often the noncustodial parent denies there is even a problem. They just don't know, because they don't work with the child on his homework or listen to him read. Again and again I've heard parents say, 'He's just lazy. He could do better if he really wanted to,' or 'Her mother just doesn't know how to work with her. I could make her get her math done correctly.'"

When special needs show up, who is going to pay the extra costs? To be sure that the child isn't left merely to limp along as best he can, the matter needs to be addressed in the support agreement or at the support hearing.

Although it is much less common, the special need may be a positive one. Perhaps the child is gifted and needs the advantages of a private accelerated school or is exceptionally musical and would prosper with private lessons. Generally such a child will not receive the same financial considerations as a child who is ill or who suffers a handicap. In fact, neither of us has seen a deviation from the basic guidelines to pay for extras for a gifted child. But that doesn't mean it can't happen.

On the other hand, your child's health is of highest importance. Be sure that you take note of any conditions that might later cause a problem. Has a doctor or school nurse mentioned any possibility of eyesight or hearing problems? Have you had reason to suspect learning disabilities or speech troubles? Has your dentist suggested that your child might need orthodontic treatment or oral surgery? Is there any sign of mental or emotional difficulties? If so, talk about it to your attorney immediately or bring it up at mediation. It is much easier to get specific consideration for special circumstances written into the support order at the beginning than it is to get that order changed down the line.

THE COST OF RAISING A CHILD

The painful fact of the matter is that when a family breaks up, it is seldom possible for either parent to maintain the family's former standard of living. The same income is there, yet now there are two households to support instead of one.

The parent who bears the greatest share of the child-raising responsibilities also bears the greatest share of the costs. Unless there is a true equal sharing of custody, the custodial parent also has less time to herself, fewer opportunities to have a break from the challenges of parenting, and fewer chances to build up a profitable career. That's why the costs of child care are so vital a part of the support picture, but unfortunately a part many parents fail to cover.

"This problem of child care is one I see over and over," Ana says. "In fact, it is probably the biggest single reason why so many women go onto welfare. Child care is so expensive in our society that if you're earning minimum wage, there is no way you can pay for it."

Nancy adds that it is such a problem that many families in mediation work out contact schedules with each parent to help minimize the need for paid child care.

But child care is just one of the many costs of raising a child that can get left out when computing support. The fact is that a startling number of divorcing parents have no idea how much money they spend on the everyday necessities and incidentals of life—clothes, food, transportation, entertainment, gifts, and so forth—nor what proportion of these costs actually go for their children.

It is vital that you make yourself aware of all of your expenses. Start a list of expenditure categories, then write down the specific amount you spend in each category. List everything. Start with food and clothes, but also consider the extra cost of a two-bedroom apartment, for instance, when you could easily get by with one bedroom if you were alone. Record the cost of utilities, the extra car expenses you incur with all the carpooling and chauffeuring you do. The cost of presents for other kids' birthday parties should be included. So should the cost of being in an organization such as scouting—the uniforms, dues, materials, and outings. List school costs, such as field trips, materials, and activities.

You won't be able to think of everything right off. Keep your list close at hand so you can jot down things that occur to you at unexpected times.

"I so wish I could send Brendan to private school," Kate said. "From the beginning of our marriage, before our son was even born, Van and I agreed private school would be on the top of our list of priorities. But now Van says he can't afford it. Is there any way I can make him help pay for private school?"

The answer depends on where Kate lives. States are divided as to whether or not private school can be considered a part of child care. Certainly Kate should pursue the matter. The judge will take into account the fact that it is something she and her then husband decided and built into their budget from the beginning. But the judge will also consider Van's income. It may be that he truly cannot afford it.

"Well, I can tell you that the amount I get in no way covers the cost of raising four kids," Janette said. "My support award isn't fair!"

"It really isn't fair that I am supporting my kids alone just because they have graduated from high school," Maxine added.

"You want to talk about fair?" Leah asked. "How fair is it that I get nothing at all?"

"If you ask me, the whole system is unfair!" Kate insisted.

Fair is a word we hear all the time from our clients. But it really doesn't fit into the legal vernacular. Many things that may not seem fair to you—or to your ex-husband, for that matter—are part of reality. Let's say your little girl wants to be an ice skater more than anything else in the entire world. And you may feel that she truly does have exceptional talent. "It's so important to her," you may plead. "It's only fair that she should be able to pursue her dream." Perhaps, but the reality is that it's highly unlikely that the court will order your ex to pay extra money for ice skating lessons, costumes, and competitions for his daughter.

This is another great example of the value of working with a mediator, counselor, or attorney. Such professionals can look at such things from an unemotional business standpoint. Since we come in as neutrals, we can examine the matter and say, "Well, I see both sides, so here is the best way to work this out."

Forget fair! Reality and compromise are the concepts you will have to live with.

WHEN DOES THE SUPPORT STOP?

"Our daughters were sixteen and eighteen when Sam and I divorced," Maxine said. "I fought hard to get all I could for them in child support. The eighteen-year-old came out with nothing, and by the time the settlement was finalized, the younger one was seventeen. She got less than one year's support. Now Sam refuses to help them at all."

In many states, eighteen is the age of majority, and thus of emancipation (the age when a person is considered old enough to be on his own). Child-support payments legally end at this age. But there is some variation among states. In Florida, the age of emancipation is nineteen if the child is still in high school. For a long time in New York the age was twenty-one.

Nancy once worked with a couple who had been divorced in New York. The father moved to Florida and the mother to

Maryland. Since the age of emancipation in New York was twenty-one, the father was paying support for his high school graduate kids, even though they were not going to college full time and had jobs of their own.

"You don't have to pay me any rent," their mother told them. "And buy whatever you want. Your father can pay the bills."

When the kids responded by spending more than was coming in on Dad's support checks, Mom came to Florida where Dad was living to fight for more support. Nancy, arguing for the father, insisted that not only should the support not be raised, but that those kids shouldn't be getting any support at all. And it wasn't because of their age. It was because they were in fact emancipated—they were not in school full time, were failing many of the classes they were taking, and they were working. To the mother's dismay, the court agreed and the support was cut off.

In a few exceptional cases it can be argued that a child under eighteen is emancipated. A child movie star who earns more money than her parents might fit into this category, or a minor who is married.

By the time Maxine was divorced, one of her daughters had already reached the age of majority and the other was almost there. If Maxine had come to either of us, we would have asked her, "Do you really want to spend the time and effort to fight for that one year of support?" Sure, the money would be helpful. But what about the emotional cost to all of you of a court battle?

Most fathers will be much more cooperative if they can see you are really trying to work things out with them. It just may be that Sam, Maxine's ex-husband, is obstinate today because of the anger and resentment that built up over those old battles.

Children with handicaps are an entirely different matter. Maybe a young person failed a couple of grades and won't be finished with high school until a year or two after she reaches the age of emancipation. Maybe a young person with a specific disability will need support for many years to come. Or it may be that he or she will need a different kind of support.

When a young person is incapacitated through illness or accident, the court rules that he is dependent because of his incapacity to care for himself. It is up to the court to decide whether or not the noncustodial parent must continue to make support payments beyond the age of emancipation.

How about Maxine's daughters' college costs? Does Sam have to pay them? Almost certainly not. But you aren't Maxine. That doesn't mean your child's college expenses won't be covered.

COLLEGE EXPENSES

Many people would agree that in this day and age a college education should no longer be considered a luxury. And, as everyone knows, college costs money, more every year. With this in mind, you would be wise to do your best to include something about college costs in your child's support agreement.

Since your child will be starting college at just about the time she reaches that magic age of emancipation, all support would come to an end unless there was something already established in writing. Written agreements for college will be enforced by the court even though the court cannot order them directly.

"There's no way Robert would ever agree to help with college!" Leah insisted.

No matter. It's up to you to bring the subject up. Let your attorney know it is important to you. Will your child actually get any money for college? We don't know. But one thing is sure: She won't get it if you don't ask for it.

A word of caution: Be careful how such additions are worded. If the clause says something about your ex agreeing to pay "reasonable expenses" your child incurs while in college, the time is sure to come when you will be asking each other, "Just what is 'reasonable'?" Such a vague term is inviting problems down the line. Lawyers and mediators should explore specific expenses, including application fees.

It's too late for Maxine and her daughters, but some college support money may well be possible for your child.

THE SUPPORT BELONGS TO THE CHILD

We talked with a grandmother the other day who was carrying her two-year-old granddaughter. Grandma was thirty-five years old.

"I'm raising my granddaughter on my own," the woman said. "Yet both my daughter and her ex-boyfriend have paying jobs. Don't I deserve some child support from them?"

Actually she doesn't, but that little girl certainly does. Child support belongs to the child and no one else—not the mother, not the father, not the grandparents, no one else. And that right to support does not stop just because neither parent is caring for the child.

"I am seeing more and more cases where the department is representing a grandmother or an aunt or someone else other than a parent," says Ana. "In those cases we bring an action against both parents. They share the responsibility."

HOW WILL THE PAYMENT BE MADE?

Child-support payments can be made in several ways, and to a large degree which method you use depends on where you live. Most people tend to assume that payments will be made directly to the person who is caring for the child. Not necessarily. In some jurisdictions the court routinely orders that child-support payments be made directly to a court officer. Arizona, Arkansas, and Kansas are three states that require all child-support payments to be made this way unless there are extenuating circumstances that call for further consideration.

There are real advantages to this payment procedure. First of all, the court automatically keeps a detailed and accurate accounting of the payments that are received and those that are still owed. If you ever have to go back to court because your child's other parent hasn't paid, you will find those records very helpful. Second, if the support is late in coming, a reminder mailed to the delinquent parent from the court is likely to carry a great deal more weight than a telephone call from you asking where the money is.

Wage deductions are another automatic form of child-support payment. While some states arrange for all support payments to be automatically deducted from the noncustodial parent's paycheck, other states allow wage deductions only when payments have been missed.

We would strongly suggest that you ask your attorney about the different forms of payment options that are available to you. If it is possible to have the payments made to the court, we would recommend it. If the payment must come directly to you, don't allow your child to be the middleman. Sure, it's a temptation for your ex to say to the kids as they are leaving his house, "Oh, by the way, give this check to your mother," but it is not a good practice. What if the check is lost? What if the child forgets to get it out of her backpack and give it to you? What if your ex insists he sent it and your child insists just as strongly that he never gave it to her? Going through the child is not only asking for trouble, it is putting an unfair burden on her.

PREPARE NOW!

"When I said I didn't want any help from Robert, my baby had just been born, and Robert and I had already broken up," Leah said. "I was a teenager living with my parents. I ate their food, charged my clothes on their credit cards, and used my allowance for stuff for the baby. But I couldn't stay a kid forever. Two years ago when I moved out of my parents' house, reality struck. Believe me, it's tough to raise a child alone. And it's expensive."

It can be really hard to look down the road and foresee what your child will need for the rest of his childhood and adolescence. If your son is just two years old, how can you know how much food teenage guys eat and how much milk they drink? If your little girl is just four, how can you know what prom dresses will cost in twelve years—or teen-approved jeans and jackets and sneakers and shirts, for that matter?

Too many mothers err by basing their support requests on what their children need right then. They don't understand that what is adequate today is certain to be inadequate in the years to come.

Some women don't ask for enough child support because they feel too guilty. They are convinced they failed at their marriage and so have no right to expect help. Others are determined to go it alone so that they can prove their independence.

But by now you know the importance of taking charge of your child's support. The question is, where should you start? We have found that the best way to begin support negotiations is to put together a detailed list of all your child's needs. Then when you sit down with your attorney, instead of pleading in frustration, "I need more money!" you can calmly pull out your list.

"Anytime you can focus on your child rather than on yourself, you have a better chance of succeeding," Nancy says.

To put off seeking the support that is lawfully due your child is a big mistake. It is especially important that any special needs be brought out before the support award is made. If you bring a matter up later, and the court decides the need was present at the time the first award was set, there is no "change in circumstances." If there is no change of circumstances, there is no reason to go back and modify the award.

A LAST WORD

You may be saying, "With the amount of money my child's father earns, I'll be lucky to get the basic child support from him. It would be a waste of time to fight for any extras."

Don't be too sure. Even though your ex-spouse may not have the financial ability to provide your child with extras right now, it doesn't mean he won't be able to do so in the future. The more you anticipate, the greater your chances of having your child's needs met in the future.

You may be surprised to find that your ex is just as concerned about your child's future as you are. Just like you, he may be confused and uncertain. Your best bet is to talk openly and rationally to both your ex and your attorney about your hopes and intentions for your child. Then write those intentions down and do your best to have them incorporated into your support award.

Write down every agreement you reach. Any agreement worth having is worth having on paper.

There is one more thing to keep in mind. No matter how great your child's needs and no matter how deserving he might be, the court cannot award him more child-support money than his other parent is able to pay. Do record every one of your child's needs, but also be ready to balance your expectations with your ex-spouse's ability to pay.

Now that you have an idea of what the laws are and how child support works, you are ready for the next step—a walk through the process.

CHAPTER FOUR

Walking Through the Process

MEET CHRISTINE. AFTER SEVENTEEN years of marriage and three children together, she and Ronald are getting a divorce.

"For the past five or six years we have been growing further and further apart," Christine said. "When I discovered Ronald was having an affair with a woman down the street, our marriage seemed too far gone to even try to save it."

Everyone agreed that the children should stay with Christine. Twelve-year-old Matthew had a really hard time with the divorce. Alexis, eight, seemed surprisingly unaffected. Little Ian, just three, couldn't understand what had happened. "He keeps asking when Daddy is coming home," Christine said. "So far I haven't been able to bring myself to say 'never.'"

Christine herself seemed philosophical about the family breakup. "It's hard and painful for everyone," she said. "But Ronald is not a terrible person, and I know he cares deeply about the kids. I really don't see any problems with the child support."

It's wonderful that Christine can maintain such a positive outlook, and we hope she is right. Yet few divorces end problem free. Any parent who finds herself in the custodial role needs to keep a firm grip on reality. As the one who is primarily responsible for your child's well-being, it is up to you to make sure you are looking realistically at the potential for problems, that you make yourself knowledgeable and aware of how best to prepare for what might be down the line, and that you act rationally and wisely.

Christine is not a typical single parent. There is no such thing as typical. But by walking through her story with her, you can get an idea of some common problems and matters for consideration you are likely to encounter along your own journey.

SELECTING AN ATTORNEY

"There is an attorney I know from church, a really nice guy," Christine said. "He won't charge me the usual amount because he is anxious to get started in his new practice here. I'm not sure how much experience he has had in the area of child support, though. I'm wondering if he's a good choice."

No, Christine, he isn't. Choosing an attorney to represent you right now may be one of the most important decisions you will ever have to make. It is vital that you make your selection as objectively as you possibly can. Your uncle is an attorney? Your good friend from high school is practicing law in your city? Your brother has a friend whose uncle will give you a good break on the cost? Great, but relatives and friends and acquaintances are not necessarily the people best qualified to handle your case.

"How about the yellow pages in the telephone book?" Christine wondered. "Surely anyone listed under Family Law Practice would be a specialist in divorce and child support."

Not necessarily. Such a listing doesn't necessarily mean an attorney has met any state bar requirements as a specialist in the area of family law. In fact, you will find many firms listed under several headings.

"Well, my friend went through a divorce last year and she had an attorney she liked a lot," Christine decided. "Maybe I'll just give him a call."

A reference from a friend is a good way to locate an attorney. But be sure to ask your friend what it was about the attorney she liked. Was his advice especially helpful? Was he knowledgeable? What specific things did he accomplish for her? Is your case similar to hers?

Before you make your decision, call the potential attorney's office to ask about a consultation and whether or not a fee is charged for it, and if so, the amount of that fee. (It is important for you to know that many of the best family law specialists do charge for an initial consultation.) When you meet, ask the attorney how many divorce and child-support cases she has handled. Ask, too, if she can provide you with references. Also check with your local bar association to see if she has a good reputation in the community. And don't hesitate to ask about her fee scale. Most attorneys work on an hourly basis rather than charging a set fee. If this attorney charges on an hourly basis, ask her if she will write out a rough estimate of how many hours the case will require and what the total cost will likely be.

"Maybe I won't use an attorney," Christine said. "I have been hearing about legal agencies that will do the same thing for a fraction of the cost, and the job will be done much more quickly."

We can understand people's frustration with the length of time it takes to get things ready for court, and we also understand the concern about cost. But we would warn Christine, and you as well, to be very careful about taking her case to a legal clinic. Too many of them are not as qualified or competent as they should be.

We hear a lot of horror stories about cases that come out of some of these legal clinics. The biggest problem is that instead of using the guidelines as a starting point, they use them as a fast and easy formula for everyone. The paper work is done quickly enough, but when the parent gets to court she may find her entire plea rejected because of incomplete personal evidence. When that happens, her chances of getting child support are ruined. When Mona went to court, she had no idea the quarterly bonuses she received at work would be included in the calculations. She was shocked to find that instead of receiving child-support payments, she would be *paying* support to her ex!

If you decide to go ahead and use such a legal clinic, make sure the person who will be handling your case is a licensed attorney. Many are just paralegals. That's not to say all paralegals are bad. It's just that you and your child's future will be better served by an experienced, well-trained attorney with a number of child-support cases under his or her belt.

"I know a woman who went to such an agency," Nancy says. "Her basic forms were filled out exactly the same way as everyone else's forms were filled out. That worked out fine for many people, but this woman has some special circumstances that should have been brought out. Her ex-husband was a brutally violent person. Yet, because that wasn't noted on the form, she ended up with a shared parent agreement. Her violent, abusive husband got the kids half the time.

"This woman was really stuck. If she were to try to go back to court and have the decision modified, the judge would say, 'Sorry, you agreed that he was fit to share the parenting responsibility. And I don't see that anything has changed.'"

Ana recalls a woman who had gone to such a service to handle her divorce. She was assured it would be a simple matter. "Just fill out these papers in the order we stacked them," the secretary told her, "and sign every place we have put a red X. When you see the judge, give him the signed papers. That's all there is to it." Then they shook her hand, wished her well, and sent her off to take care of everything alone.

Feeling confident, the woman filled out the papers and signed beside all the red Xs—including a petition stating that no children had been born of the marriage. A bit concerned, the woman called the clinic and pointed out that she and her husband had three children.

"It doesn't matter," she was assured. "This form will make your divorce go through a lot more smoothly. And don't worry, after the divorce you can get your child support through the social service agency."

The woman went to court and got her final judgment of

divorce. Then she came to Ana about getting child support for her three children.

When Ana looked at the order of divorce, it clearly stated that no children had been born of the marriage. "You *have* no children with him!" Ana told her. "It says so right here. How can I now go before the court and say you do when you swore you didn't? In signing this form, you have made your children illegitimate. I'm sorry, but I can't get any support for them."

The distressed woman cried, "What can I do?"

All Ana could tell her was to get a private attorney and see if he could have her order of divorce set aside.

"A mistake is not so hard to go back and change," Ana says, "but her signature on that form was an out-and-out lie."

"But I'm broke," Christine cried. "I don't have any money for an attorney. I have no choice but to find a clinic that will take me on a contingency basis. That way I won't have to pay until I get some money."

Fortunately, Christine does have some choices. First of all, she needs to understand that sooner or later, if she uses the services of a legal clinic, she will have to pay. And the price could be close to the amount she would pay an attorney.

One alternative would be to seek the services of a mediator who can work with both parents. If you can come to an agreement without going to court, you can save both the cost and the emotional wear and tear of a court battle. Use the same method to find a good mediator as you would to find a good attorney. Get specific references from friends, call the local bar association, and talk with the mediator on the telephone.

Another option is the government's social services program. Again, you won't get the personal attention a private attorney or a mediator will give you, but you will get accurate information and professional handling. And it will cost you next to nothing. It is possible that you might qualify for legal aid. To find out, call the bar association in your county.

When Christine's father offered to pay her attorney fees, Christine selected a woman who had a good deal of experience with child-support cases. The first thing her new attorney did was advise her to make a comprehensive list of all Ronald's financial assets, his income, and information on his lifestyle.

TAKING INVENTORY

"Ronald isn't a bad guy," Christine told her attorney. "I mean, he will be open and honest about what he can afford. I'm sure of that."

Maybe and maybe not. Unfortunately, in most cases an ex-spouse will be concentrating more on looking out for himself, which means he will be inclined to be forgetful when he is listing his own assets and will tend to minimize what he has available to him. And many will play games with their deductions in order to manipulate their net income. That's why it is extremely important that you make a comprehensive list of everything you know about his finances, including his *gross* income.

When you get to court, the judge will base his decision on what your attorney presents to him. And the only information your attorney will have to work with is what you have given her.

If you have as much information as possible with you when you first sit down with your attorney, it will save you time. And since you will probably be paying her by the hour, it will also save you money.

"So what assets should I look for?" Christine asked.

Good question. To start with, here are some specific questions to answer about your ex-spouse's earnings:

- ▼ How much money does he make?
- ▼ Does he get routine raises in pay?
- ▼ Does he have stocks and bonds through his company? (Many companies allow employees to participate in voluntary investment programs.)
- ▼ Does he have a payroll savings plan?
- ▼ Does he get bonuses or commissions?
- ▼ What insurance benefits does his company provide,

including medical, dental, and life insurance?
- ▼ What other perks are available, such as a car allowance?
- ▼ How much control does he have over the amount of his bonus?

Use your answers to begin your asset file. Here are some other things you should add to that file:

- ▼ Life insurance policies
- ▼ IRA and 401-K accounts, and pension funds
- ▼ Real estate holdings
- ▼ Stocks, bonds, and mutual funds
- ▼ Personal property (including jewelry, antiques, cars, boats, electronics, and so forth)
- ▼ Any money that is owed him

To your list, add any other financial information, including:

- ▼ Copies of all the income tax returns you filed during your marriage
- ▼ Your ex-spouse's social security number
- ▼ Any credit cards he has and their numbers (including credit cards you had together)
- ▼ All bank, savings and loan, and credit union accounts along with the account numbers
- ▼ Outstanding debts he has incurred, including mortgages
- ▼ Anything else that could possibly have any bearing on his financial situation

In addition, Christine should prepare a budget for her expenses as a single mother.

"This is hard," Christine admitted. "Ronald always took care of our finances."

That's in the past. It's time to change all that. Start by writing down everything you do know. Then list all the professionals your ex-spouse deals with (or dealt with during your marriage) who might have more information—people such as accountants, bankers, attorneys, stock brokers, and business associates. These are people who may be able to give you information you need.

There is one more list you should add to the asset file: a description of lifestyle matters that were a part of your family's life while you were married, or that you and your ex-spouse had agreed upon together. Examples might be music lessons, summer camp, private school, travel plans, specific organization memberships, college, or a child's wedding.

When Christine had gathered all her information together, she took it to her attorney. After looking over the lists and records, her attorney asked, "Tell me, Christine, just what is it you are hoping for in child support?"

"I want the kids and me to be able to live like we did before the divorce," Christine told her.

"Do you work outside your home?" her attorney asked.

"Yes, I have a great job at a little dress shop," Christine said. "I go in around ten or so, after the older kids are in school and Ian is in preschool, and work until around two. It's real flexible, so if something else comes up I can work less or not even go in at all."

"How much do you earn?" the attorney asked.

Christine laughed. "Not that much," she said. "Actually, I take almost nothing home. I end up using my pay to buy clothes. It's a great deal, with my employee's discount and all."

Christine had a lot to learn about the realities of child support. As we have seen, very few people are able to live as well after the divorce as they did before. There just isn't enough money to go around. It is extremely unlikely that Ronald will voluntarily support Christine's old lifestyle of working part time when it fit into her schedule, then spending all the money she made on clothes for herself. It is even more unlikely that a judge would order him to do so.

Christine's attorney knew priorities would have to be set. She started out by congratulating Christine on being so thorough in gathering together all the necessary information.

"I was afraid I had brought a lot of stuff that wasn't all that important," Christine admitted.

"It's much better to have too much than too little," her attorney assured her. "If we don't need it, we won't use it."

Christine, with her attorney's help and guidance, set about establishing clear and realistic objectives for child support. She could go to work, at least half time, Christine conceded— and not at a place where she would spend her entire paycheck. She wanted music lessons for the two older children, and she wanted Ian to continue at the private preschool he had been attending for the past year. She wanted Ronald to handle all the medical and dental bills, including the orthodontia Alexis was sure to need. And because Matthew was having a hard time in sixth grade, she wanted him to attend a private school when he started junior high. She also added summer camp for the children and special tutoring for Matthew to her list.

When the objectives had been set down, the attorney had Christine rank each point according to its priority. The medical and dental costs ranked at the top. Ian's preschool ranked high, as did the tutoring. Summer camp came in near the bottom, and Christine conceded that the music lessons were something she could probably pay for herself if she needed to.

"Maybe I should just leave music lessons off the list," she suggested.

"No," her attorney insisted. "At this point, put down everything. You may not get it all, but one thing is sure—if you don't ask for something, you have no chance of getting it. No one will be offering you anything."

A phrase Christine's attorney emphasized was: "*If* he has the ability to pay."

"You can add this to any of the provisions you and Ronald agree on but that he cannot now afford to pay, such as Matthew's private school," she told Christine. "Ronald is a draftsman in business for himself, and who knows, his income just may go up. You can also apply this phrase to things that will be coming along in the future, such as college for the kids or Alexis's wedding."

Things may get better. They sometimes do, and as Christine's attorney emphasized, you should be prepared for that. But you should also be prepared for problems down the road.

ANTICIPATING PROBLEMS

"Tell me more about Ronald," Christine's attorney said. "What is he like?"

The attorney wanted to determine if there were character or behavioral traits in Ronald that might alert her to problems in the future. And who was in a better position than Christine to know? The attorney asked, "Does Ronald pay his bills on time? How is his credit? How important is his credit rating to him? Does he buy on impulse? Does he have large debts on his credit cards? How does he work out his debts: Pay them off promptly? Play games with the people he owes money? Pretend like the debts don't exist? Argue and stall? Depend on you to rescue him?"

"Why all the questions about debts?" Christine asked.

"Because," the attorney said, "from now on, you are another one of his creditors."

"Well, he did sometimes get behind on the bills," Christine conceded, "but we're talking about his children. They will be at the top of his list of priorities."

Don't count on it. Whatever your ex-spouse's financial behavioral patterns, they aren't likely to change. Just as you are now worrying about how to get by on less money and still lead a fulfilling life, your ex-partner is—or soon will be—doing the same. He, too, will have only a certain amount of money, and he, too, will have to set down priorities.

If you see the makings of a problem down the line, be sure to talk it over with your attorney. There may be clauses she can add into your settlement to minimize the risk.

When everything was arranged, the child-support award was made to everyone's satisfaction. And for the rest of the year, everything went along just fine. Ronald seemed to truly enjoy his time with the kids, and his payments were always right on time.

Well, Christine thought, *this hasn't worked out so badly.*

WHEN PROBLEMS ARISE

Around Christmas the children started talking about Joan. "She's Daddy's lady friend," Alexis said. Matthew smirked and raised his eyebrows in a way that showed his admiration of Joan's physical attributes.

In February, the support check was late. Only a few days, but late nevertheless. The March check was even later, and April's check didn't come at all. Ronald still visited the kids every other week, but he didn't take them to his apartment anymore. And when Christine called to ask him about the check, she learned that his telephone had been disconnected.

When Christine confronted him the following Saturday, her suspicions were confirmed: Ronald had moved into Joan's house.

"And the support check?" Christine demanded.

"I'm trying," Ronald said. "But I've got a lot of expenses now."

Joan had children of her own, Christine learned, and Joan's ex-husband wasn't paying any child support at all. "What am I supposed to do?" Ronald asked. "Her kids have to eat. I'm doing the best I can, Christine. You've got to be patient."

But it's hard to be patient when you can't pay the bills. "How do you expect *us* to live?" Christine demanded. "Moving in with your girlfriend was your idea. Anyway, her kids aren't your problem. You have kids of your own to worry about!"

In the weeks that followed, Christine learned a few more things about Ronald's new living situation. When he moved in with Joan and her children, he took over the rent on her apartment as well as the payment of the utility bills. He was also paying for Joan's son's after-school football.

Ronald finally made his April child-support payment, but from then on the checks were consistently late. In September, the month he married Joan, the check didn't come at all.

Christine had had it. "Ronald insists he'll make it up to me later," she told her best friend. "But without that check, I can't make the mortgage payments. He says he just needs time to get on his feet. Well, what about my feet? The children and I need that money, and we need it on time!"

At this point, Christine had several choices. She could either go back to the original attorney who already knew her case, or she could seek out a new person to represent her, or she could go to the department of social services for help. Because she was out of money, she chose the latter.

When Christine signed up for an appointment, she was told, "I'm sorry, but the first available time we can set you up with a caseworker is three weeks from tomorrow." Christine took the appointment.

Three weeks later, Christine was given a stack of forms to fill out. Then she had a twenty-minute interview with a caseworker whose parting words were, "I'll do my best, but I can't promise you anything."

After that first interview, Christine waited to hear something from her caseworker. While she waited, Ronald continued to stall. "Next month for sure," he promised. Then, "Things will be looking up soon." But still no money. Christine continued to wait. The bank called her about her overdue mortgage and reminded her that the late penalties would be costly. She had to borrow money from her parents to pay the electric bill and buy food. And still she waited.

"One of the worst things about waiting is having to listen to everyone's advice," Christine said. "Mom says, 'I told you not to marry him.' Dad says, 'This wouldn't be happening if you had gone back to the lawyer instead of going to that service center.' My sister says, 'You shouldn't have asked for so much from him. You scared him off.' A coworker says, 'Be sure you get my uncle's friend's cousin for a judge.' My neighbor says, 'My girlfriend got an income deduction order. You should have gotten that.' I'm sick of all of it!"

Eventually Christine got a notice in the mail telling her to appear in court. The waiting was over.

At court Christine finally met the lawyer who would represent her and had a chance to talk to him. "Maybe we can settle this matter before going to the hearing," her attorney said.

Actually, 40 percent of the people who show up at court do settle without ever having to go inside. Unfortunately, it didn't work that way for Christine.

YOUR DAY IN COURT

Christine's case went before a hearing officer rather than a judge, a growing practice in many states that helps prevent the judges' dockets from becoming completely clogged. Sitting next to her attorney, Christine looked up and saw Ronald across from her, sitting alone.

"Why doesn't he have a lawyer?" Christine whispered to her attorney.

"Most likely a tactic," he whispered back. "Ronald figures he'll gain sympathy points if the hearing officer thinks he's too poor to afford one."

When he caught Christine's eye, Ronald gave her a look she knew so well. She could almost hear the words: "What did you drag me here for? This whole thing is so ridiculous!"

In many states, including Florida, all Christine has to show is that there was support ordered and Ronald has failed to pay. Then Ronald has to explain why he couldn't pay, and his reason had better be exceptionally good.

"I have to think about Joan's kids now, too," he told the hearing officer. "What am I going to do, let them go hungry and be in need?" The court took a dim view of Ronald's priorities, and he was found in contempt of court and ordered to jail.

At the time Ronald was sentenced, he was assigned a $2,000 "purge amount" (the amount he will have to pay in order to be released from jail). Ronald was fortunate. The court could have demanded he pay the entire amount of his debt. Whatever the purge amount, the hearing officer must find that the delinquent parent has the present ability to pay that amount. If the parent doesn't have the money, he must be able to raise it quickly—by selling his motorcycle or a watch, for instance, or cashing in some stock. The court usually won't require him to do anything that will cause him undue hardship, such as selling his house or selling the car he uses to get to work. (It can require him to get a loan against the property, however.)

Within hours Ronald's wife showed up with the $2,000. Like most people, he paid the purge amount. Joan had sold their second car to get the money.

On the way out of the courtroom, Christine beamed at her attorney. "Well, that's all settled!" she exclaimed.

"Yes," her attorney replied. "At least until next month."

Basically, Christine was back at square one. If Ronald falls back into his old pattern, she will have to start all over again.

"If Ronald had not been in business for himself, Christine could have asked for an income deduction," Nancy says. "That way the child support would be automatically deducted from his paycheck and sent to the clerk of the court. Then the clerk would send it to Christine."

What if the father changes employers?

"The custodial parent would still have the income deduction order," Ana says. "All she would have to do is send a certified copy of it to his new employer."

That's fine if there is an employer, but what about Ronald and Christine's case? Is there something similar for a parent who is self-employed?

"He can still have an income deduction against him, and he still has to honor it," Ana says. "It's just a lot harder to enforce when there is no employer."

Many custodial parents think that if their ex doesn't pay, he'll automatically go to jail. The fact is that most delinquent parents never are jailed. It's not uncommon for a delinquent parent to go before the judge and plead, "I'm going to pay, I promise. It's just that I hit some hard times and I got a little behind." Even though the judge finds the delinquent parent in contempt of court, she may say something such as: "All right, I want you to pay $100 in thirty days." Or she may say: "Pay your ongoing child support on time and include an extra $20 on every check until the debt is paid up."

"When Ronald stopped paying, I was afraid he had no work," Christine told her attorney. "I guess this all would have been a lot harder then, wouldn't it?"

If Ronald had nothing, there would be nothing for Christine to get. Child support is not a punishment. In this country we don't have debtors' prisons where people are locked up until they pay up. All the court is doing is trying to collect the money so that the child can be supported properly. If the money is there, they will collect it. If it's not there, they won't.

MOVING ON

By now you may be saying, "That all sounds like an awful lot of work!" It is. But we can't emphasize enough the importance of educating yourself in every aspect of your case. It can make the difference between quickly getting the support your child needs and deserves, and floundering for months—even years—while you wait for someone to take you by the hand and lead you through the maze. You started out feeling help-less and confused. Now is the time for you to say, "I can do this! I can take the responsibility. And for my child, I *will*!"

A TIME FOR EVERY SEASON

As wise King Solomon wrote in the book of Ecclesiastes: "To every thing there is a season, and a time to every purpose under heaven. . . . A time to get, and a time to lose; a time to keep, and a time to cast away; a time to tear, and a time to sew; a time to keep silence, and a time to speak."

One night several months after Christine's day in court, her parents asked her, "Why are you spending so much time with your child-support files? The matter is settled. Ronald is paying on time now."

"I don't know," Christine said tentatively. "I've been

thinking about other things I should have asked for. I'm wondering if I shouldn't start thinking about getting the award modified. I mean, Alexis really wants to take gymnastics this year. And Ian is almost old enough to start thinking about soccer. And Matthew. . . ."

For some women, the divorce and the issues surrounding it become a full-time, all consuming job. It literally takes over their lives. They spend so much energy gathering and organizing materials, so much effort discussing the "ins and outs" and seeking advice, so much time poring over every bit of information they can get their hands on, that when the end is in sight they can hardly bear to see the matter settled. It has become their life, and they just don't want to give it up.

Clearly the time has come for Christine to let go and move on with her life. It may be that some modifications to the child-support award will indeed be appropriate down the line, but now is not the time and these are not the circumstances.

Moving on means making specific decisions and acting on them. For example:

▼ Stop allowing the divorce to be the center of your conversations. Your friends and family will appreciate it, and it will do you and your children good to begin to focus on other things.
▼ Let go of your anger and resentment, and be willing to forgive the past.
▼ Let go of your dreams of what might have been. Now is the time to take hold of what is, and make it as good and positive as you possibly can.

Some emotions can be dealt with simply by understanding them and where they came from. Other emotions are not so easily overcome. In the next chapter, we will be talking about the emotional impact of divorce and child-support battles.

▼ ▼

CHAPTER FIVE

The Emotional Impact

MAGGIE AND LOUIS, both levelheaded professionals, have been divorced for a year. They now live across the country from each other. Theirs is a somewhat open-ended shared custody arrangement, but their constant fighting makes it next to unworkable. For instance, last Christmas both parents bought nonrefundable airplane tickets to take the children on a two-week Christmas vacation—Maggie to ski in Colorado, Louis to visit his parents in South Carolina. The result was tears, accusations, disappointments, and even more hostility than before.

Today their sixteen-year-old daughter states, "I don't want to be with either one of them!"

It's a strange thing about divorce. People who are basically loving, kind, considerate, and rational often behave totally out of character. They act in ways they never have before and probably never will again. Usually calm, controlled people suddenly lash out in angry tirades. They become suspicious and distrustful. They plot, accuse, and blame.

"I know I can be unreasonable," Maggie conceded, "but I just get carried away. I am consumed with this desperate wish that things could be the way they used to be with us, that everything wasn't over. Then I hear his voice or read a note from him and I go out of control."

It's unusual to have someone admit it. More often people insist they are fine, that it is their ex who is out of control. That certainly is how Louis sees it. "She is a crazy woman," he says of Maggie. "Everything she does is done for spite. There isn't a kind bone in that woman's body."

The truth is that both Maggie and Louis have let their emotions take over, and they are both out of control.

Unfortunately, at just the time you are dealing with some of the most important issues you will ever face, you are also struggling with emotional upheavals. You need to know that such emotions as guilt, anger, hurt, revenge, resentment, and remorse can seriously affect your ability to make wise decisions.

"That's just great," you may be saying. "I wish I could put off my legal problems until after my emotions have settled down. But you just finished advising me to get on with the process. I can't put off things like arranging for child support."

That's very true. And this is the reason we think it is absolutely essential that you gain enough insight and understanding about what is going on both inside and outside of yourself—and that you discover enough ways to work within your stressful situation—to keep you from making serious errors.

Perhaps the most serious error of all is to drown your children in the flood of your emotions. Your kids are already burdened down with their own heavy loads. When more is piled on—such as having to choose whether to go skiing with Mom or to visit Grandma and Grandpa with Dad—it is just too much to bear. What you put on your kids now will affect their emotional development. And how you handle your emotions will impact your relationship with them for years to come.

Because our focus is on caring for the children, let's first consider our children's emotions.

THE IMPACT ON THE CHILDREN

What does divorce mean to kids? Here is what some children who have seen it firsthand have to say:

"It means I have to choose which parent I will love most."

"It means I can't play Little League baseball any more."

"It means if my ear hurts I just have to let it hurt because we can't afford to go to the doctor."

"It means I can't be a kid anymore. I have to be the man of the family now."

Like their parents, children of divorce experience disbelief, anger, fear, anxiety, confusion, guilt, resentment, helplessness, loneliness, depression, and more. These emotions are magnified in children who must also endure ongoing hostility between their parents. As Maggie and Louis's daughter shared, the hardest thing of all is having to choose.

Why should you cooperate with your ex? The answer is easy: for your child's sake. When both parents work together for a child's good, that child has a far better chance for a healthy, secure, and satisfying life. When parents cooperate, it usually follows that both parents have better relationships and fewer conflicts with their child. There are fewer problems with visitation and child support and less fighting between the parents. And since the child can't help but see the spirit of cooperation and the sharing of responsibility between his mother and father, the cooperation serves as a wonderful example for problem-solving in his own life.

"I don't know," Maggie said when the value of cooperation was stressed to her. "Louis and I couldn't get along as husband and wife, so I don't think we could ever get along now."

Don't believe it. They can get along, and so can you—for the children's sake.

What kind of things are especially damaging to kids? Here are a few of the worst:

▼ Not allowing them enough quality time with both mother *and* father.
▼ Threatening to send the child to live with the other

parent if she doesn't behave. ("I'll pack your suitcase for you!")

▼ Using the child as a messenger to carry angry notes back and forth.

▼ Stressing how bad (mean, unfair, dishonest, unloving, uncaring) the other parent is.

▼ Making the child choose between his parents.

▼ Not letting the child know what is happening or what to expect.

▼ Burdening the child with adult problems. ("I'm so afraid we won't have enough money to pay the rent this month," or "I'm sure Dad is having an affair.")

▼ Looking to the child for strength and comfort. ("You are the man of the house now. I know you will take care of me," or "I want you to pick out which apartment we move to.")

"Well, there's one fortunate thing," Maggie said. "At least our kids are doing well. The fourteen-year-old is angry, but that's just part of being a teenager. The eleven-year-old is just fine. It hasn't affected him at all."

Dr. Judith Wallerstein has done a great deal of research on the children of divorce, following children for fifteen years after their parents split up. She found that while most people insist their children act and behave as if the divorce is not harming them at all, there is sometimes what she calls a "sleeper effect" where the damage shows up only much later. This is particularly true in girls. It shows up in higher high school dropout rates and higher levels of teenage pregnancy. Later on it shows up in broken engagements. After they marry, it shows up in problems in their own marriage relationships.

If children cannot get their emotional needs met in their families, they are likely to grow into adults who have a hard time making commitments to long-term relationships. They harbor a real fear that they could end up like their parents and cause their own kids the same pain they suffered. Again and again we hear people say, "I'm not going to have any children, because what if I ended up getting a divorce? I won't put my children through what I had to go through."

Nancy says, "Still, so many people say, 'But the kids are fine. They never talk about the divorce, and they are doing well in school.' Unfortunately, that doesn't necessarily mean all is well. The children could be having real problems that they are keeping carefully hidden, or they may suffer effects down the line."

The teacher of a gifted class told about journals her students kept every day. They wrote down their thoughts, concerns, ideas—anything they wanted. The journal entries could be shared with the teacher or kept private as the child saw fit. Amy and Michelle, two students in the class, were both children of divorce. Amy shared openly and matter-of-factly about her family and her life at each parent's house. There was little conflict between her mother and father, and Amy obviously felt a great deal of love from and for each parent. She seemed to feel comfortable in both homes.

For a long time Michelle didn't show any sign of wanting to share her journal. Then one day she asked her teacher if she might read a bit to her. What Michelle shared was a great deal of conflict and stress. "Everything hurts somebody else's feelings," the ten-year-old wrote. "And my brothers and me aren't allowed to talk about anything we do at my dad's house because then my mother will find out stuff, like what things he has bought and how much money he has."

Both Amy and Michelle did very well in school. Neither seemed to show other signs of problems. There was nothing to alert anyone that Michelle was living with such stress. She didn't talk about it to anyone, except that one teacher that one time.

Even in children like Michelle, the stress is likely to show up in negative ways, very possibly during the volatile teen years. And the odds are that it will continue to haunt them in their future male/female relationships.

Don't depend just on what you see and hear from your child.

Understand that the emotional conflicts are there, and do all you can to make it as easy on your child as you possibly can.

"YOU'RE MAKING OUT LIKE A BANDIT!"

"Maggie has really got it good!" Louis complained. "She has a great job, I keep the kids half the time, and I still give her money for child support. She has nothing to complain about."

"Louis has no clue about anything," Maggie countered. "I don't earn nearly as much as he does, and although he keeps the kids half the time, I'm the one who gets stuck with all the extra costs. Just last week I had to buy a costume for our youngest for a school play. And the week before that, our oldest gave his first party, and guess who paid. Right! Me. Louis is the one who has it good. He gets all the joys of parenthood with few of the responsibilities."

When people are struggling with their emotions at the same time that they are trying to adjust to their new standard of living, it is awfully easy to look over at that other parent and build up fantasies about how well the ex is getting along.

Is it true? It doesn't matter. The only relevant truth is that this new life is going to take a good deal of compromise and adjustment. Don't allow yourself to cling to the fantasy that everything is wonderful over there and if there was any justice in the world all would be well for you, too. That's only a fantasy that allows you to avoid reality.

So what is reality? For the great majority of divorcing couples, the reality is that both mother and father have to learn to get along on much less. And because of the way our society operates—specifically the inequitable pay received by women as compared to men—it will be much harder for the mother to rebuild her life than it will be for the father. That is reality.

The thing to do is to focus on *managing your affairs as best you can*, work toward putting your life back together using the resources available to you, and refuse to waste your precious time and energy on fantasies about what your ex's life is like.

NOTHING BUT A WALLET

"I don't mind supporting my children," Grant said. "But I have no intention of supporting their mother. I mean, I send her this support money every other week. Then the kids come to visit me dressed in worn out, outgrown clothes, and hungry because they haven't had anything to eat but dry cereal and canned macaroni and cheese. I feed them and I buy them clothes. So why am I paying out this support money?"

We hear from fathers like Grant all the time. "I'm nothing but a wallet!" they claim.

Certainly there are mothers who abuse their support responsibilities. But a greater problem is the men who don't understand all that is involved in supporting a child. They think only of expenses directly related to the child, such as clothes and food. But there is also rent—without the kids she wouldn't need that extra bedroom. And there are utilities—kids use a lot of electricity and gas and water. There's the telephone bill—no explanation needed. And automobile expenses—chauffeuring puts a lot of miles on a car and requires fuel in the tank. And you have to count the dinners at McDonald's drive-through—after working all day and going straight to take Susie to ballet class there is no other way to get dinner for her before she has to be at church for choir rehearsal.

"I hear this so often," Nancy says. "In mediation, we look for creative ways to explore children's budgets. The thing is to demonstrate as clearly as possible that the money is going to the children, not to their mother."

A father who falls into the higher income category recently told Nancy he felt that the guideline amount he was paying was wasted. "No money is being set aside for my children's college education, and after paying such a large amount, I can't do it," he said. "I can't even buy them clothes!" Nancy helped the parties negotiate a college savings fund for the children, and Dad is now included in clothes shopping trips. Everyone is more satisfied with the arrangement.

"It really steams me to have to pay money directly to

Ellen," Grant said again. "She only considers me the kids' father when it's time to collect money. She never consults me about anything concerning them. She took our oldest to the orthodontist last week and never said a word to me. I would like to have been there for the consultation, too. Ellen doesn't even invite me to the kids' school open house or to their music recitals. I'm locked out until it's time to pay."

When Grant and Ellen first separated, he pulled away from the rest of the family for a while. "I had to be alone so that I could get myself together," he explained. "Until I got myself straightened out, I couldn't do anything to help the kids."

It was almost three months before the children saw their father again. He did send money, but not on a regular basis. And all that time, Ellen struggled on alone in her new role as single mother.

"Grant says he needed time to himself," Ellen said with more than a trace of bitterness. "Well, good for him. But what about me? I was left with the kids and the responsibilities and no idea if there would be any money for the bills or not. Now he wants to be included in everything. Well, all I can say is, 'You did a good job of proving we could get along without you, and now we're doing just fine, thank you.'"

But Grant sees it differently. When Ellen gave him the bill for his daughter's ballet lessons, he handed it right back and told her, "You enrolled her in ballet without a single word to me. So now you can pay for it."

Grant does have a point.

"It's not always a matter of anger and revenge," Ana points out. There are also times when people are looking at the arrangement from a totally different viewpoint.

The culture in which a man was raised also influences the way he behaves toward his ex-wife and children. In some cultures, having an ex-wife who has to go to work is taken as a personal affront. ("Everyone will think I can't take care of her.") Other cultures see children as property, and the property goes to the father. For such a man, it is demeaning, an embarrassment, to have his children in the custody of their mother. These are things you must consider if you are ever to see the situation through the father's eyes.

Sometimes it is the mother who is bound by culture and the father who cannot understand. Some women feel, "I can't go to work. A mother's place is at home with her children. I have to raise them. Their father will just have to come up with the money to support us all."

In general, fathers have five major complaints:

1. It doesn't take nearly as much money to raise a child as the guidelines say it does.
2. I write the checks, but I have no control over how the money is spent. There is no accounting of what the money actually goes for.
3. I don't like being ordered to pay for our children's support. I would happily pay if I wasn't ordered to.
4. I am not included in the decisions that concern my child.
5. Even though it is called child support, I feel that what I'm really paying is alimony to my ex-wife.

Some of these complaints are valid, and some are not. The reason many men feel the guideline figures are unfairly high is because they think about the amount it took to raise their child in an intact family where there was just one rent payment, the utilities were paid once, and everyone ate together. It is true that many difficulties could be lessened if custodial parents would be more candid about how the money is spent. And it is valid for noncustodial parents to expect to be included in decision-making that affects the child. As for fathers willingly paying child support, research does not bear that claim out.

So what can you do to help your ex feel that he is more than "just a wallet"? Here are some suggestions:

▼ Be sure to include him in your decision-making regarding the child.
▼ Make sure he knows about your child's activities. Give

him enough notice so that when it is time for t-ball sign-ups, he can be there. Not only will he feel included, he will also see the price-tag on the uniform, hear how much the team picture will cost, and be told how often your child will have to bring the orange juice.

▼ Ask him his opinion on matters that involve the child. You don't have to follow his advice. Just asking will go a long way toward making him feel involved. And who knows, he may come up with some great ideas.

▼ Think of him as your child's other parent, and allow him to do some parenting, including such activities as clothes shopping.

"This will be hard for us," Ellen said. "Grant and I hardly speak."

You don't need to speak. When he comes to pick up the children for their visit, leave him a note: "Vicky's game will be next Saturday at nine o'clock. She would be happy to see you there." Or you can have a parenting notebook, which you pass back and forth with your ex, for written communication.

Sometimes the noncustodial parent's anger and resentment run so deep that he cannot be a part of the parenting. "I'll quit my job before I'll pay a penny," he might threaten. Or, "I'll leave the country. If I have to suffer, you'll suffer too!" A person's anger can be so overwhelming that he just doesn't care about anything else. He'll use his children, he'll leave town, he'll give up his career just to get back at the other parent. When a parent's emotions get this far out of hand, there is little you can do but determine that you will be the best, most supportive parent you can possibly be.

Some custodial parents respond to their own pain by turning on their ex.

"I'LL MAKE HIM PAY!"

"My ex cheated on me. Now it's payback time! My goal is to clean that man out. I don't want him to be able to walk in his front door without regretting what he did to us."

"If my ex-husband doesn't pay his support on time, he won't see his children. I won't allow him any contact with them at all."

In anger and frustration, and hurting badly from the divorce, some custodial parents lash out with threats such as these. It's a terrible approach.

Taking revenge by making unreasonable demands is a tactic that seldom gets results and very often backfires. If the child-support payments are oppressive, chances are that in a short time no payments at all will be made. It's not uncommon for the noncustodial parent simply to take off. When that happens, everyone loses: mother gets no child support, father has no contact with his child, and the poor child gets it from both sides—no support money and no daddy.

As for the threat of withholding contact with the child if the support is not paid fully and promptly, in most states this is against the law. It may seem like the easiest weapon to use, it may even seem fair to you, but stop and think about it: Not only would your child suffer, but you would be buying more trouble for yourself in terms of ever being able to work out a cooperative payment plan with your ex.

"I use this tactic, but I do it subtly," Loretta insisted. "When my husband comes to pick up Todd, I say he's sick. Or I call my ex's house when he's at work and leave a message on his answering machine saying that Todd will be going to a birthday party and can't make it on Saturday."

"I let our daughter decide whether she wants to go with her dad," Ruth said. "All I have to do is smile sweetly and say, 'It's up to you, dear, but the rest of us are going to Disney World.' It works like a charm."

"I lay the groundwork ahead of time," Bobbi Jean said. "I tell my teenagers, 'Oh dear, Saturday is your day with your dad. But that's the only day I can go to the mall with you, and I wanted to get you some new things. Oh, well, I guess it can't be helped.'"

Very clever. But also terribly damaging.

"In Florida we have a rule that says a parent has an affirmative obligation to ensure a continued relationship with the child," Nancy says. "Subtle or not, children cannot be kept from their parents."

"But," you might say, "my child really doesn't *want* to go."

Generally, this is not a matter for your child to decide. Instead of saying, "Do you want to go?" say, "This is the day you go." If the child argues, you might point out, "This is your dad's time to be with you."

If your child continues to resist, you need to take steps to find out why. It is not normal for a child not to want to see his parent. It may be simply that your actions and attitudes are influencing him. But it could also be a more serious problem. This would be the time to consult a counselor.

"Kids need both structure and sensitivity," Nancy points out. "They are already going through a hard time. It should not be made tougher by expecting them to make big decisions, especially ones that are sure to displease someone."

Your child has the right to be supported financially, and she has the right to love and enjoy both her parents. It is easy to get these two rights tangled together, but they are two separate issues. One thing has nothing to do with the other. If your ex lives across the country and hardly ever gets to spend time with your child, your child still has a right to financial support. And, however much it rubs you the wrong way, if your ex fails to make his child-support payments for a week, a month, or even a year, your child still has the right to spend time with her father.

The very best you can hope for your child is that he will continue to enjoy a healthy, loving relationship with both of his parents. You can play an important part in seeing this come about. Sometimes it may seem like too much to ask, but your constructive and mature behavior will go a long way toward helping your child get the love and security he needs.

INTIMIDATION AND GUILT

"I don't wear something new when I might see my ex-husband or he will think I am using the kids' support money on myself."

"I have a good job and a good salary. Maybe I really shouldn't be getting money from him."

"He has a new family now, and he feels they should come first."

"He tells me he doesn't like the way I'm raising the children. He says if I'd do a better job with the kids, he wouldn't mind paying support."

"He says he will be happy to take the kids and let me write out the support checks."

These are the thoughts and feelings that intimidate you and cause you to be consumed with guilt. Some of them may be simply your imagination working overtime. But many are likely built on comments you overhear from your ex, intimations you read between the lines, things the children tell you he said—or actual statements he makes to you.

Many comments spring from an ex-spouse's attempts to rationalize his opposition to making the support payments. That's his problem. For you, the danger lies in believing his accusation, especially if there is so much as a grain of truth in it. That's when the guilt comes creeping in.

For some people, the guilt starts at the very beginning of the divorce process. "The split was my fault," some women say. And feeling responsible, they want little or nothing in the way of child support from their ex-spouses. Even when their attorneys insist on asking for more, some will insist, "No, I really don't want it. It wouldn't be right."

Whatever stage of divorce and child support you are in, keep this warning firmly in your mind: *Do not let your emotions do your thinking for you.* It will cause you to make decisions that are not in your best interest and, more importantly, that can be devastating to your child.

Manipulative people can be excruciatingly hard to deal with, yet in the end it's up to you to prevent yourself from being manipulated. Your ex may threaten to tell your child that you are trying to ruin him. He may insist that you are bankrupting him. He may say you are living high while he is struggling to scrape by. He may accuse you of being cruel or unfeeling or selfish or un-Christian. He may even insist that you are a bad mother. But you know the truth about yourself and your motivations. That is what you must cling to.

Intimidation is only useful if it is effective. If you refuse to be intimidated, if you move ahead parenting the very best way you know how, and if you allow the law to help you do things properly and in order, you and your child will be the ones who benefit.

COMMUNICATING WITH YOUR EX

"Randy needs braces," Maggie said as she sat in Nancy's office.

"He does not," Louis argued. "He looks just fine the way he is."

"You are so cheap!" Maggie shot back. "You don't care about the kids at all. What about Paul? He needs medication for his hyperactivity, but you have fought it all the way."

"I do care a lot about them!" Louis insisted, his voice rising. "But you don't seem to care what things cost. For your information, I'm not made of money. I can't afford braces and medicine on top of all the money I already shell out!"

When Nancy, acting as mediator, was finally able to quiet the battling couple and to help them look over the materials they had brought her, she discovered that both Maggie and Louis had health insurance through their employers.

"They were so busy fighting, they never bothered to communicate," Nancy says. "They had no idea whose insurance covered what."

Once Nancy got them calmed down enough to look at their policies, they discovered that Maggie's policy would cover Randy's orthodontic work and Louis's policy would cover Paul's medicine.

"Then the answer was easy," Nancy recalls. "Maggie took Randy's bills, sent in the insurance forms, and paid whatever amount wasn't covered, and Louis did the same for Paul's prescriptions."

Few families fall right along the predictable lines. They

always seem to have some exception to the norm. Most people do much better when they look for creative ways to work together to give their children the best care possible. When parents cannot, or will not, communicate with each other, their children lose—and so do they.

"My ex is impossible to work with," Ruth stated. "He is the most irresponsible person to ever walk this earth. He would never remember to send in insurance forms for the kids."

Personalities do make a difference. You know your ex-spouse's strengths and weaknesses, and certainly you will not want to cause even more problems by placing unrealistic expectations on him. Still, the tendency is to assume the worst. We constantly hear people say such things as, "He was late on Saturday to pick up the kids just because he wanted to be sure to ruin my weekend." And we respond, "Are you sure? He might have overslept, or maybe he got stuck in traffic." Assuming the worst puts a huge stumbling block in the communication process.

So does speaking in absolutes. "He is *always* late picking them up." *Always?* Really? Or is it possible that it just seems that way to you? Absolutes put the other person on the defensive, and it is awfully hard to communicate when you are busy defending yourself.

Another barrier to communication is making assumptions and placing blame. Some people think there is money where there is none. They say such things as, "I'm sure he got a good raise because I saw him driving a new car." His ex has no idea that he was actually driving his boss's car. Men will say, "She doesn't need money from me because her grandfather is going to leave her a bunch of money in his will." Maybe he is and maybe he isn't, but how is she going to pay this month's rent? A man might say, "Why should I pay? Her family is wealthy." So what? Her family isn't responsible for the children. The children's two parents are.

If fears and suspicions aren't talked about, then the truth cannot be known. If the truth is not known, the inflated fantasies will be carried around forever.

Many of these misunderstandings are understandable and don't arise from one person trying to destroy the other. It is just that the two parents are looking at the matter from different points of view. If they can come to the place where they are able to communicate, they will find that both truly want what is good for the children. Neither wants to take advantage of them.

"A mediator can do a lot to help people communicate," Nancy says. "A father might say, 'She is asking a ridiculous amount from me. It doesn't cost that much to raise a child.' I would respond, 'I hear you saying that you feel your children could get by on much less. Would you go home and make a list of all the expenses you think relate to your child and give me a copy?' Then I tell the mother, 'I would like you to do the same.' The next time we meet, we look at the two lists and see where they differ. Seeing it written down in detail helps people understand the realities.

Again, outside professionals can help come up with creative options to sticky problems.

"Jay tries to make me look bad to the children," Loretta stated. "Days with Dad are always fun days—amusement parks, water slides, snow skiing. Days with Mom are boring—after I buy shoes and groceries and other essentials, there is no money left for fun and I am out of energy anyway. Meals with Dad are restaurants and takeout. Meals with Mom are plain old nutritious stuff. I hate being the boring one while he gets to be the exciting one."

"What am I supposed to do?" Jay asked. "I live in a small apartment with a roommate. You have the house, remember? And as for meals, I don't know how to cook."

A mediator can come up with other possibilities, such as taking the kids to the mall and letting them spend their allowance, or going to a movie, or going to museums, or playing baseball in the park. If it actually is true that Dad is trying to show up Mom, then the mediator can help the two deal with that as well.

If you and your ex are committed to working out your problems, you might try sitting down together and talking through some tough spots on your own. The trick is to be as nonoffensive as possible. You might say, "I can understand that it is difficult for you to have the kids at your apartment. But when you take them to all those expensive places, it makes it awfully hard on me. Would you consider taking them to the library or the park or on bike rides most of the time and saving the expensive places for special occasions?" This technique uses "I" messages and focuses on one's own feelings. It is much less defensive than a "you" message.

You may find that he is totally unaware that there is a problem. He may even be relieved not to have to keep up the spectacular outings that are putting a real strain on his bank account.

If you decide to work together without an outside mediator, be careful to make use of good communication skills. Stay with the "I am feeling" statements rather than the "you shoulds." Stay away from the judgmental and the accusatory and the defensive. If things begin to break down, take a time-out. And agree that if you just cannot make it work, you will seek out a mediator.

Working together as parents means cooperating with each other on all matters that have to do with your children. It makes no difference whether you get along or you can't stand each other. Working together as parents means working out and carrying through on a parenting plan that gives your kids the chance to be loved and cared for by both of you. Working together as parents means sharing the responsibility for your children, respecting each other's parental rights, and refusing to invade each other's privacy. And it means working out a way to communicate about matters that have to do with your children. Working together as parents means giving your children the physical care and emotional health that will allow them to become the best people they can possibly be.

RESPECT THE CHILDREN

If you allow your negative thoughts and feelings—your anger, resentment, and bitterness—to remain, they are going to grow into hatred. It will damage you, and it will damage your child.

Please, please, do not bring your child to court. It serves absolutely no purpose. If we think a parent is going to be found in contempt and be sent to jail, we insist that children be removed from the courtroom, even if we have to have someone take them to the snack bar for an ice cream cone.

Yet we often have women say, "No, I want them to stay. They need to see this!" Those children do not need to see it. Insisting that they do is nothing but revenge, and it wreaks havoc on the kids.

Many parents seem to assume that their children are deaf and dumb. They sit and discuss their anger and frustration with friends or family members, detailing the partner's every sin, while the kids are right in the next room. "Oh, he's not paying any attention," they will say. Or, "She's not interested in any of this." Of course he is paying attention, and certainly she is interested. Those are their parents that are being discussed in the next room. And the kids are terribly affected by what they hear and observe.

Fifteen-year-old Annette summed up her emotions this way: "I'm not really concerned with the money. And I don't want to know about all the problems. I just want to have a mother and a father."

Doesn't your child deserve that much?

▼ ▼

CHAPTER SIX

What If We Were Never Married?

JESSICA WAS SIXTEEN WHEN her baby daughter, Lily, was born. "I know I'm young and still in school and everything, but Brad's older and settled down," she said. Brad, Lily's father, was nineteen and did minimum-wage janitorial work in an auto supply store.

"We talked about getting married, and we still might, but Brad isn't sure he's ready to settle down yet," Jessica said.

"My parents wouldn't pay my hospital bill from when Lily was born," Jessica continued. "They told me that was Brad's and my responsibility. There was all the money I owed the obstetrician, too. My parents wanted me to take Brad to court to make him pay, but he and I decided that would be silly. We would have to hire lawyers and everything. Brad paid some of the hospital bill, but there is still a lot to go. He hasn't paid any for quite a while."

Jessica had not planned on being a single mother at sixteen. All through her pregnancy she talked about allowing her baby to be adopted, but at the last minute she changed her mind. "I couldn't stand the idea of not seeing her grow up," Jessica said.

One out of every four children born in the United States today is born outside of marriage. What used to be considered rebellion has now taken on the trappings of an acceptable lifestyle. Gone are the stigmas that used to keep things "in line."

Many babies born outside of marriage are the products of people living together. "We're seeing situations where a woman has two or more children all with different fathers," Ana says. "Many of those women are very angry because they feel cheated by their partners and overwhelmed by the system."

When such women come for help, their cases are especially hard, because we can't do anything for them until we locate the child's father.

It would seem that we as a nation are reaping what we have sown. And it is having a catastrophic effect on our children.

It very quickly became apparent to Jessica that babies are a lot more expensive than she had imagined, what with diapers, clothes, formula, and all the special equipment they require. The bills were piling up, and Jessica had no money.

When Jessica put pressure on Brad to help with some of the expenses, he dragged his feet. "He says he doesn't think he should have to pay the hospital bill, and certainly not the money to the doctor," Jessica said. "He does give me five or ten dollars now and then for diapers and stuff, but it's not nearly enough. And my parents won't help me anymore. They say this baby is my responsibility, not theirs."

Broke, alone, and going further into debt every day, Jessica applied for government help. She was given Aid to Families with Dependent Children (AFDC), Medicaid, and food stamps. Now she was yet another statistic—one more teenage mother on welfare.

With taxpayers looking more and more disapprovingly at the expanding welfare rolls and their soaring costs, in a case like Jessica's the local social services office steps in and files an action for paternity. The purpose is to see that fathers like Brad pay to support their children.

Jessica was assigned a caseworker, Mrs. Bowen, who immediately tried to contact Brad. She had no success. An investigator found that Brad had moved from his apartment and left no forwarding address. At the auto parts store, he was informed that Brad had quit abruptly over a month before.

They had no forwarding address either.

Using their location services, it did not take the social services office long to find Brad. He was still in town and working at another job. Brad was promptly sent a summons.

"He won't argue," Jessica assured Mrs. Bowen. "He knows he is Lily's father."

"Good," Mrs. Bowen said. "In that case we can go right on to the final hearing, establish paternity, and pick up the support on the same day."

Unfortunately, Jessica was wrong. "That baby isn't mine," Brad insisted. "Sure, I dated Jessica, but so did lots of other guys. No way am I paying bills and support for someone else's kid!"

"What do we do now?" Jessica cried.

Mrs. Bowen's answer was simple: "We establish paternity."

ESTABLISHING PATERNITY

For children whose parents are not married, one of the most serious barriers to getting child support is failing to establish paternity. Besides helping to get children off the welfare rolls, establishing paternity also provides them with important medical history, and it gives them the right to inheritance and government benefits.

Although not all state requirements are the same, in Florida, AFDC recipients are legally required to cooperate in identifying and locating the alleged father. But any woman, even if she isn't on welfare, can apply to the Child Support Enforcement Office to help her establish paternity. If this service would be helpful to you, call your local social services office to see what is available in your state and what requirements or conditions apply.

Statutes in some states specify that in any paternity case, blood testing must be provided if either the mother or the father requests it. Florida has a contract with a licensed national laboratory that allows us to have this testing done at a reduced cost.

"I don't think Brad will have the blood test," Jessica said

when she was approached with this suggestion. "He won't be able to afford it."

First of all, Brad won't have a choice in the matter. He will be ordered to cooperate with the test. And while it is true that the testing doesn't come cheap, he won't have to pay for it. The state will usually pick up the cost. Only if he is found to be the father will he be required to reimburse the state.

As she was waiting to hear the results of Brad's blood test, Jessica called Mrs. Bowen. "This will be the end of it, won't it? I mean, if the blood test comes back positive, Brad can't argue about being Lily's father—can he?"

"Well, a positive result on the test would be pretty persuasive evidence," Mrs. Bowen agreed. "But the paternity ruling still isn't automatic. If Brad has a very good story, he might insist on taking the matter before a jury."

There have been some cases where a man's explanation was compelling. One young man insisted, "I'm sterile and have been for the past ten years." Another stated, "I was in prison at the time she got pregnant. Check the records." Another argued, "My girlfriend was also sleeping with my twin brother." Blood testing can be extremely accurate, but in rare cases it is not conclusive.

States differ in what they consider conclusive evidence of paternity. In Florida, when the blood test results show a statistical probability of paternity of 95 percent or higher, the test is considered a "rebuttable presumption," which means a matter is presumed to be true or accurate unless convincing proof to the contrary is presented. Florida law allows the Court to establish paternity based on the testimony of the mother in addition to that 95 percent or greater probability.

If there is still question after the blood test, DNA testing can be used. Here the accuracy level rises to 99.99 percent. A positive result here doesn't leave much room for argument!

In many states, a man who contests the paternity judgment has the right to a jury trial. Florida has recently gone back to recognizing that right. Yet there have been very few jury trials for paternity. The evidence of the blood tests and other DNA tests are too compelling.

When Brad's blood test came back, the results were positive. In the light of the evidence, Brad conceded, "Yeah, I'm the baby's father."

If he hadn't agreed, the court would have listened to his argument as well as Jessica's, then would have considered the blood-test findings. In all probability, after weighing all three, they would have ruled that Brad was indeed Lily's father.

"This isn't fair," Brad grumbled. "I'm only nineteen, and here I am stuck with supporting this kid for the next eighteen years! I mean, it's not like I forced myself on Jessica. Why should I have to pay?"

Because, Brad, you fathered the child. Men must begin to understand that if they decide to be sexually intimate with a woman, they had also better be ready to accept the responsibility that may follow.

"I wish young men, especially those in high school, would be required to witness these paternity proceedings," Ana says. "I would like for them to see firsthand the consequences of irresponsible sexual behavior. I'm convinced that many would come out of the courtroom saying, 'There but for the grace of God go I!' And hopefully their actions would reflect more responsible behavior from then on."

"I do think we have more of a movement toward abstinence in this country right now," Nancy adds, "at least in certain circles. The fear of AIDS has contributed to this trend."

FOR WHOSE BENEFIT?

More and more we see the concern of the court turning toward the best interest of the child. Take for instance a case here in Florida. A married woman had a child by a man other than her husband. Even though she was still married and living with her husband and their children, she wanted to bring a paternity action against the man who had fathered her baby. The Supreme Court of Florida said that if she did that, they would appoint an attorney for the child to look out for her best interest.

The court's point was that it may well not have been in the best interest of the child to declare her illegitimate. Why take her away from her legal father in order to find a new father for her?

Far more common are couples like Patty and Darryl. Patty had been married to a man named Frank. Although they separated years ago, they never legally divorced.

"It's just like we are divorced, though," Patty insisted. "I haven't even seen Frank for years and years. I can't even remember how long it's been."

Patty is wrong. Separation, even long term, isn't just like a divorce.

Patty came for help because Darryl, the man she had been living with for the past five years, left her when their baby was born and refused to help her support the child. "Darryl is my baby's father, and I need money from him," Patty said.

Yes, but the law says Frank is the baby's father because he is Patty's legal husband.

"But I haven't even seen Frank for years."

Still, legally Frank is her husband.

"But we are separated."

Separated is not divorced.

Can anything be done to help Patty? Yes, but it won't be easy. She needs to serve Frank with legal notice of the action so he has an opportunity to object to the action.

"I don't think Frank will cooperate," Patty said.

If not, the court will have to bring in an attorney for the child, and that attorney will have to be paid. In order to sort out each person's relationship, including the child's, and try to determine what is best for the child, the attorney will have to interview everyone who is in any way associated with the case. Then comes the blood testing to legally determine paternity. Regardless of what the mother says, both men will have to be tested.

"That makes no sense at all," Patty insisted. "I haven't been with Frank for seven or eight years, and my baby isn't even a year old!"

Frank may still need to be tested.

"It's way too expensive," she insisted. "And everyone will tell you that Frank couldn't possibly be the baby's father!"

It's true that the testing is expensive. But it still has to be done.

Frank had his own opinion. "I don't have anything to do with this whole case," he said. "I have been leading my own life hundreds of miles away from Patty and her relationships. Why should I get involved? I refuse to be tested."

Frank doesn't have that option. Without a legal divorce, he is that baby's father until it is ruled in court that he isn't. And that won't be done until the paternity is determined with a blood test.

Both Patty and Jessica were the mothers of very young children. Most people we deal with are. But what about a mother who didn't get child support when her child was a baby? Can she go back and do it later?

IS IT EVER TOO LATE?

When Mary Grace discovered that she was pregnant, she was just starting her senior year in high school. She married Anthony, she said, "just to make the baby legal." They never even lived together. Anthony gave her money now and then, but after graduation they divorced, he moved to the next town, got remarried the following year, and Mary Grace lost touch with him.

"I have done okay," Mary Grace said, "but it hasn't been easy. Teddy, my son, is now ten, and I really want to go back to school. I could do it if I could get some child support from Anthony. But now, after ten years, is it too late?"

If Teddy were no longer a minor, it would be too late. But since he is only ten, Mary Grace can still file on his behalf. Whether or not she will get the support she requests depends to some degree on which state she lives in.

"My friends say I should really get ten years' worth of support money for my son," Mary Grace said. "I mean, I had to struggle to lay out the money Anthony really should have been paying all along."

Don't plan on collecting that money from years past. Very seldom does such an award include much, if any, retroactive child support. Most likely all Mary Grace can hope for is support from the time she files (now, when Teddy is ten) until he reaches the age of emancipation (eighteen in most states).

Still, it wouldn't hurt to try. Things are changing. Again, the question is not fairness to the mother or the father, it is what is in the best interest of the child. In 1991 in the District of Columbia, the court held for the first time that child support should normally be awarded for a child born out of wedlock unless there is a good reason why the father should be relieved of his obligation to contribute to the support of his child from the moment of its birth. In reaching this decision, the court cited recent decisions in Massachusetts and Florida where retroactive child support was awarded.

Sometimes mothers file for child support years later, and when the father is notified he claims, "I didn't even know this child existed. This is no time to tell me. I can't even be a father to him now."

The father has a point. All those past years are lost to him. If the child is more than twelve years old, he won't even have the opportunity to have much input into the child's life. In some states, the court will not award child support in cases like this unless there are some very unusual circumstances.

David Levy, a fathers' rights advocate, stresses the importance of allowing fathers to be a part of their children's lives. To the argument that men are more likely to make good on their car payments than on their child-support payments he says, "When you make a car payment, you have the car. But after making a child-support payment, the odds are fifty-fifty you'll ever get to see the child."

The main thing to remember is this: It is far better to get the child-support award as soon as the other parent is no longer living with and supporting the child. But if it is already too late for that, then the best time to do it is *right now*. Better sooner than later, but better later than never.

"Well, so far my mom and dad are really supportive financially," you might say. "As long as I know I can always come back later, I think I'll hold off and see if I really need that support enough to make it worth getting involved with my baby's father."

Understand that by waiting, you are doing yourself and your child a great disservice. We repeat, the best time to pursue support is immediately.

The matter of determining paternity is a sad and frustrating one. We wish we never had to deal with this at all. Yet there is a large segment of our society in which teenage pregnancy is considered acceptable. And it is also considered acceptable for the men who fathered those children to take no responsibility for them. "She wanted another kid," a twenty-year-old father said. "She gets more money from the state if she has two. So I've actually done her a favor."

Perhaps this is just an extension of the attitudes of our society as a whole. In many, many areas we have ceased to call people to responsibility. The catch-phrases of our day are:

"It's not my fault!"

"I'm entitled to it!"

"Someone else should fix this."

"Someone is going to pay!"

Perhaps the place to start fixing the problem of paternity and unwed pregnancies is to work at fixing our families and our homes.

CHAPTER SEVEN

▼ ▼

Today's Complex Families

LESLIE WAS A FORLORN little girl. Her faded clothes, always either too large or too small, were obviously hand-me-downs. Quiet and withdrawn, Leslie could usually be found tucked into a corner, reading a book, her cat Puff curled up beside her.

When Leslie was eight years old, her mother decided she'd had it with barely scraping by and never having a life of her own. She was tired of being a poor single mother. So she packed Leslie's meager belongings into two shopping bags and drove her across town to where Leslie's father lived.

When Leslie's father came home that evening, he found Leslie sitting on his front step, her shopping bags beside her and her cat on her lap. Pinned to her shirt was a note that read: "Gary, I've had Leslie for eight years. I'm ready for a life of my own. Now it's your turn to take her. —Fran"

Gary had remarried, and his new wife was not at all pleased with this addition to the family. Space wasn't a problem. The house was spacious, so there was plenty of room for Leslie. Money wasn't a real factor either. Gary was a prosperous architect, although they did manage to spend whatever he earned. But he and his wife Arlene had two-year-old twin sons, and Arlene saw this bedraggled girl as an imposition on her tidy life. Besides, how would she ever explain the girl to her family and friends?

93

"She doesn't belong here," Arlene insisted to her husband. "Anyway, we can't afford her."

"Maybe if you hadn't made such a fuss about my paying support she wouldn't be here," Gary retorted.

Leslie sat in the corner of her new room, snuggled her cat, and cried.

It used to be that when most people thought of a family, it meant a mother, a father, and a couple of kids. Today, "family" includes single parents, stepparents, kids from a previous marriage, and an assortment of grandparents past and present. Some families can get downright complex and confusing.

Too often, along with the complexities come resentment, jealousies, recriminations, hurts, insecurities, and neglect. The complexity also raises a lot of questions. If a man has two families besides the one he is living with and he is short of money, which children get priority? If a man is struggling to meet the support of his families, yet he is planning to start yet another family, what consideration does he get in his support obligations? If a man who is paying support for his children from a former marriage marries a woman who is paying support for her children, does their marriage affect the support payments of either? Hard questions, and whatever the answers, someone is going to be unhappy and feel cheated.

Some people say, "We should look at it as if it were first and second mortgages—priority goes to the first." Others insist, "The priority should go to the present family. Too much stress on them will likely spell doom for that family, too."

The answer is, the first priority is the best interest of all the children.

People tell us, "The problem is men who continue having children they can't afford. Why does a man start a new family when he knows the cost is just going to exhaust the amount of money he has to live on?" We ask the same question, and we have no answer for it. Even so, every one of those children deserves as good a quality of life as he or she can possibly have. And that father has a responsibility to them all.

EMOTIONS MAKE A DIFFERENCE

"Gary's responsibility is to me and his sons," Arlene insisted. "I realize Leslie is his daughter, but that part of his life is past. His ex-wife is a selfish whiner who uses any support money she gets on herself. It's sad, but it is not Gary's fault. And it certainly shouldn't be my problem."

Emotions play a huge role in how the various families fare. It is impossible to separate the child support from how the parents and children feel about the divorce.

Arlene had never been married before. When she married Gary, she saw their family as being made up of the two of them and the children they would have together. She knew about Leslie, of course, but Leslie didn't fit into the family Arlene had in mind. And anyway, she reasoned, Leslie belonged to her mother, not her father. Since the day Arlene married Gary, she resisted any support for or contact with the child.

When both partners in a marriage have been through a divorce, usually with one paying child support and the other receiving it, they are more accepting of the support money and the visits because they both know firsthand how the arrangement works. It is when one partner has never had children before that problems are especially prevalent. The new wife sees the support money being paid out, but since she has never been on the receiving end, she has less compassion and sensitivity about it.

Ana went to court with a woman who had not received her support checks for months. When we got into the hearing room, the woman's ex-husband was already there with his present wife. He came over to Ana's client and said, "I can't understand why you are doing this. I have sent you a check every month."

"I haven't gotten a check from you for five months," the woman told him. "I can barely pay the rent and buy food."

"I wrote the checks myself," the man insisted. "Look, here's my checkbook. You can see the dates, the check numbers, everything."

"All I know is that I haven't gotten any money and the kids and I are really hurting," the woman said.

It wasn't until after the hearing that the man's new wife stepped forward and admitted, "I didn't mail those checks. I'm really sorry, but I just couldn't stand to see all that money going out."

She had let her husband go to court; she had heard him swear under oath that he had paid the support. He was on his way to jail for contempt of court, before she said anything.

"How could you do that?" the man asked his wife.

"I just thought we needed the money more than they did," she said.

It can be hard to make ends meet, and many families really do have to stretch and even do without. We don't deny that. But that does not change the fact that by assuming other obligations, a parent by no means cancels his obligation to that earlier child or children. Their needs do not decrease.

WHAT PART DOES ALIMONY PLAY?

People often confuse alimony and child support. Many times we hear people say such things as, "He should have to pay me alimony—or child support, or whatever you call it." Please understand that alimony and child support are two very different things. Alimony is money given to a former spouse for his or her support; child support is money given for the support of a child.

It used to be that people who made child-support payments would call it alimony on their tax returns because alimony would get them a better deduction. Then in more recent years a ruling came down from the Internal Revenue Service that said in essence, "If it looks like child support and it smells like child support, we consider it child support, and you won't get the alimony deductions for it." Perhaps this history explains some of the confusion between the two terms.

In mediation, child support and alimony may be mixed in order to maximize dollars to the family and minimize dollars to Uncle Sam. Also, it is important to know that alimony can be used in the income-sharing formula of child support.

Alimony isn't awarded in every divorce. To a large degree, it depends on such things as how long the couple has been married, the health of the husband and the wife, and each person's ability to earn an income. Some states, such as Texas, don't have alimony at all.

"Can I get the social services department to help me collect the alimony I am owed?" you might ask.

No, you can't. That agency does not get involved in collecting alimony unless child support is also owed.

"What if my ex files for bankruptcy? Will that get him out of having to pay support?"

The answer to this question may surprise many people: Should the person who is paying support go into bankruptcy, neither alimony nor child support is canceled. There can still be a problem, however. Let's say Jim is making alimony payments to Jane and child-support payments for their children, but he is behind on both those payments. If Jim files for bankruptcy, Jane cannot file an action on the overdue payments. The action is blocked until the bankruptcy is settled. It doesn't cancel the debts, it just delays the inevitable. But in the meantime Jim cannot be found in contempt or be put into jail for not paying. Jane just has to wait for the money. The good news is that when the debt is finally paid, it can be with interest.

PRIORITY THEORIES

Charlie has two teenage children by his first wife. He has another child by his second wife. With his third wife he had two more. He just married last year, and now has a new baby daughter. As a manual laborer who earns $10 an hour, how can Charlie possibly pay support for his five older children and still provide any kind of a home for his wife and baby? Ask a group of people, and they will come up with several different answers:

▼ He should support his new family. (And ignore the older children? That doesn't seem right.)
▼ He should support the older ones. (But what about this family? He can't let them go hungry.)
▼ He should divide the money up among all the kids. (Then no one would get enough to do any good.)
▼ He should let them all go on welfare. (That is exactly what we are trying to avoid!)

Even among the professionals who decide such things, there is a lot of controversy, argument, and indecision on this issue. Yet priority is an important question to consider. It comes up again and again and again. Different states are looking at this issue in different ways, doing their best to hit upon an approach that is as fair as possible to everyone. Yet, as of now, the matter of previous children is addressed in the guidelines of only a few states.

Basically there are two methods of determining support payments in the complex families of today. When an action is brought, the court can consider all the parent's children who are under court order, then divide up the guideline amount accordingly. Or it can consider only the children whose support is being determined at that specific time and ignore the rest of the kids.

Let's see how this would work in Charlie's case. Karla, Charlie's third wife and the mother of two daughters, takes him to court to force him to pay support for their children. If the court uses the first approach, it will take the guideline amount, divide it up six ways (he has six children, remember), and send Karla the payment for two children. If it chooses the second approach, the court will consider only his two children by Karla, and an amount would be set for them.

Even if the second approach is used, Charlie has a responsibility to support his other children. If he is paying court-ordered support for them, he can deduct those payments from his net income before the support for Karla's children is calculated. Under both state and federal law, there are limits to the amount of other support that can be deducted. That limit can make it pretty hard for someone like Charlie who has so many support obligations.

What if Charlie insists he just cannot meet the support requirements of the guidelines? After all, money can be stretched just so far. In that case, Charlie can argue in court that he needs to have his support responsibilities adjusted downward, but it will be up to him to prove that it is indeed necessary. The court will not deviate from the established guidelines unless Charlie can prove to its satisfaction that his financial obligation to his present wife and new baby affects his ability to help support his and Karla's daughters.

Sound confusing? It can be! And the hardest part of all is trying to be fair to everyone.

"IT ISN'T FAIR!"

How can we possibly be fair to everyone? We wish we had a good answer to this question. But the fact of the matter is, there is no way to be truly fair. Child-support awards are not always fair. Life isn't fair. Still, insensitive as it may sound, when you are working toward establishing support for your children, your own kids need to be your number-one concern.

When we handle a case, we maintain that previous families are not our business. Some people may think this means we don't care about those others. We do care. It's just that it is our job to do the best we can for the family we are representing. That is the approach you can expect from your attorney as well.

If you are remarried and your spouse has other support obligations, encourage him to keep up his responsibility to those children, both in terms of money and in terms of personal contact. Even though it may affect your own standard of living, make it an iron clad rule that you will in no way attempt to undermine your spouse's relationship with his children. But also be true to your responsibility to your own children and to the support they deserve from their other parent.

The "It's not fair!" cry is one we hear frequently in court, and often it has nothing to do with too many children to support. "I can't pay," a man might say. "Just look at all these other expenses I have!" And often the judge will reply, "Maybe you should have thought about your responsibility to this child before you committed yourself to a $300 monthly car payment."

One man came to court to appeal his support settlement arguing that it was unfair and he couldn't possibly pay it. When his financial affidavit was presented, we saw that even though he was behind on his $20 a week child-support payments, he was managing to pay $25 a week for the maintenance of his dogs. He was paying more for dog food than he was in child support, yet he was crying, "Unfair!" He could afford to support his pets, but he could not afford to support his child.

SORTING IT OUT

When you look at the jumbled background of ex-spouses and stepchildren, it can be pretty scary to try to figure out just where you fit into the picture. You may be afraid of losing your important place in your child's life. Please understand that you can never be replaced. Your child may be very fond of his new stepparent. His relationship with his stepfather may be blooming. Sometimes it may seem that they are all he talks about. But please know that *you can never be replaced in his life*. More than anything else, he needs the consistency and love and understanding you give him.

You say you can't believe it? You say all the assurance in the world can't calm the doubts and jealousies that plague you? If your insecurity is causing you real discomfort, it would be a good idea to get a wider perspective of your situation. It may help to become involved in a support group with other single parents where you can share your concerns and learn from theirs. Or it might be wise to consider a few sessions with a counselor. It will be worth the money it costs to be able to come to terms with your doubts and fears and to find reassurance concerning your own value in your child's life.

The best and healthiest thing you can do for your child is to give him permission to love all the people in his life and to receive the love each of you has to give him. Like you, he needs every bit of love he can get. Encourage him to honor and respect his other parent and his stepparent as well as you and not to take sides when there are disagreements between any of you.

It may be hard for you to see now, but your child's stepparent truly can fill a special place in his life. She can be a friend in a way neither you nor his father can. You do not need to compete with her, because you are not vying for the same role. You are his mother. She can never replace you.

However complex your family, you can rise above the confusion and set a healthy standard for open acceptance and love for your child.

CHAPTER EIGHT

▼ ▼

Making Changes in Support Amounts

"MY LITTLE BOY IS LIVING with my ex-husband," Maria explained through her tears. "I miss David so much, and I worry about him every day." According to Maria, her ex-husband, Lloyd, was a violent person. He could be very kind and charming, but when he got angry, he would fly into an unpredictable rage.

How did it happen that Lloyd had custody of their son?

"I agreed to it," Maria said. "Lloyd told me if I didn't let him have David, he would convince the judge I was an unfit mother and I wouldn't be able to see my son at all. He can be very convincing. I agreed out of fear, and I've regretted it ever since."

That was four years ago. Now, Maria insisted, Lloyd's violent outbursts were becoming more frequent and more severe. "I am so frightened for my son!" she cried. "But I don't know what to do."

Maria's was not a simple case. The boy, it turned out, was not living with his father at all. Lloyd had given him to his paternal grandmother to raise. This was particularly frustrating for Maria since Lloyd had recently gone to state services to have the support amount increased and was giving none of it to his mother for David's benefit.

When Lloyd was contacted about the boy's welfare, he

angrily insisted, "I have custody of him!" And legally he did.

An important thing to understand about divorce, custody, and child support is that nothing is permanent. Everything can be changed if there is a good enough reason. What is right and best for the child at one time may not be right and best months or years down the road. It is preferable to cover all the possible contingencies when the agreement is first set, but that is not always possible. Unforeseen changes do arise.

Some states have programs where the two parents can go before a mediator and attempt to talk out problems that come up. But this is a relatively new provision, and not every state has standards and licenses for mediators. Even in states that use them, not all courts order people to mediation. Many parents aren't even aware that this option exists.

An acquaintance recently told Nancy, "My ex has lost his job and started a new business. He says he is going to reduce my alimony and the child support he pays for the kids. The thing is, he still manages to maintain a big house and a fancy car. If he reduces the amount he pays for very long I'll be out working a second job to make up the difference. What should I do if he goes ahead with his plans?" Perhaps a closer look should be taken at the new business. One of Nancy's former clients discovered that the salary her ex was taking as president of his new company was only 25 percent of the salary being paid to his new wife as receptionist for that company. Personal businesses have a great deal of control over salaries and perks for all employees.

Nancy suggested the woman hire an attorney or go to mediation.

"An attorney would cost me more than I would be getting in alimony," the woman told her. "Anyway, he has already told me he isn't hiring an attorney. He's going to take care of this himself."

Nancy suggested a mediator, and the woman and her ex agreed. The woman was afraid that if she allowed the alimony and child support to be reduced for a period of time, her ex would get used to the lower level of payments. Then, when he got another job or his business improved, he wouldn't want them raised back up. She feared she would be forced to hire an attorney to deal with that.

"I hear your concern for your future security," Nancy told her. As an option, Nancy suggested a way to use the alimony provisions in the tax law. The ex could pay a larger amount of alimony and less child support and still have less out of his pocket because it would be money he wouldn't have to pay to Uncle Sam. Another option would be to get together annually to make decisions about levels of income and support.

Another concern this woman had was that her ex wouldn't work very hard in the new business. He objected. Nancy suggested they share a regular listing of the business he was undertaking, when he was hired, and so forth.

"What I tried to do was give Maria and Lloyd options through mediation," Nancy says. "I was convinced that both of them would accomplish more there than they ever would in a courthouse."

Can changes be made in child-support orders? Absolutely! But it by no means happens automatically. To receive an upward modification in the support your child is getting, you will have to prove that one of the following is true:

1. Your child's needs are greater than at the time of the award, and the noncustodial parent has the ability to pay more for support.
2. The existing child-support order is simply not adequate.

But here is the "catch": In both cases there must be proof of a "change in circumstances" since the entry of the original child-support order.

STANDARD FOR MODIFICATION

At this time, it doesn't seem that any state has come up with a reasonable process for periodic modification. While the

Federal Support Act of 1988 has called for a process for reviewing orders every three years, many states have yet to comply. Even though no one is requesting anything, the Child Support Enforcement Agency is supposed to look at each order periodically and compare it with the current guidelines. If it has gone up or down the agency should call the person involved to come in. That's what the law says. In actual practice, it isn't usually done because no one has the time to do it.

Yet an automatic review can be important. "Here is another place a mediator can be helpful," Nancy says. "You can agree that every several years you will come in to see a mediator, sit down with your income tax returns, insurance policies, and other documents, and review your support agreement together."

Standards for modification vary from state to state. Modifications can be quite difficult depending on the laws of a particular state and the ability of the custodial parent to prove the change. For instance, in Florida, the courts have generally used a 10 percent increase in income as the minimum for considering a change in circumstances. That means that unless the noncustodial parent is making at least 10 percent more, the court will not recognize a substantial change—even if the child is older and costs more to raise.

Another problem is that the burden to prove the change is on the petitioning party. The custodial parent must have direct knowledge of an increase in income, not just the fact that her ex has a new house and drives a new sports car. It must be fairly certain that there has been an increase in income before the action for modification is filed.

A downward modification is in order when one child no longer requires support—when she moves out of the house, graduates from high school, reaches eighteen, or gets married.

"My ex and I could do the downward adjustment ourselves," you might say. "I mean, if we have three kids, the support would just be reduced by a third, wouldn't it?"

Maybe and maybe not. A quick check of the guidelines will show that they aren't set up that way. The expenses incurred by two children would not be a third less than those incurred by three children because some things remain constant—the cost of the house, for instance. Other things, such as utilities, would decline, but not by that much.

"Then how much less would it be?"

That is impossible to predict, because the judge would have the final say. But you can get a pretty good idea by looking at the guidelines for two children. Of course you and your ex's incomes may have changed by that time as well, and that will make a difference.

In the nineteen years Jason had been employed by the same company, he had advanced so that he was earning three times what an engineer usually makes. Then suddenly he was notified that he was being laid off, a victim of downsizing. Jason was a good engineer with a great deal of experience, and his references were superb. He could easily find another job. Only trouble was, he would have to accept much less pay.

So Jason went to court to get a reduction in the child-support payments he was making. "My job is gone, and I won't be getting it back," he told the court. "Now my pay is just half of what I was earning. I doubt that I'll ever earn such a high salary again."

Jason is entitled to a downward modification. The previous child support was based on an income he no longer has. The only thing his ex-wife could do would be to prove that his income reverses are not permanent or that he voluntarily left his job. Otherwise, Jason has a perfectly valid claim.

Alan, too, filed for a downward modification on the grounds that he was earning considerably less money. He had gotten into a fight with his boss, and in an angry huff had stomped out shouting, "I quit!"

"I was sure I could get another job right away," Alan said. "I am a good worker. It's just that I had an unreasonable boss. I guess I had no idea how bad the job market is. The truth is, I can't find a job that pays nearly as much. If I had it to do over again, I would stay where I was."

It was a tough break for Alan. But his was not an involuntary change. His support was not modified.

Tom, too, requested a modification because of a change in income. "All of us at the plant were let go, then we were offered our jobs back at less pay," he said. "Some guys really got hit hard, but I was one of the luckier ones. Still, I am now making 5 percent less than I was earning. That's why I need to have my child-support payments reduced."

Not only must the decreased income be involuntary, it must also be substantial. Judges don't look kindly at people who come to court over little bits of money. Tom should be able to absorb a 5 percent reduction in his income.

Support for LeeAnn's children was set before her state had guidelines. She simply sat down and figured up a budget, then she said to her ex-husband, "You will have to pay $75 a week."

But now there are guidelines in effect. Recently LeeAnn was talking to a friend who said, "I'm getting $250. How come you're getting so little?"

LeeAnn went to the public library and looked up the statute that governs child-support guidelines in her state. She discovered that instead of $75 a week, she should be getting $200 a week.

"No way!" her ex said when she told him about the difference. "We have an agreement. You can't change it now."

Is LeeAnn entitled to a modification in her child support? Again, it depends on the laws of the state where she lives. Under current Florida law, she is. Here, if the guideline amount is 25 percent more than what a person is receiving, then that person may be entitled to a modification, even though there is no change in circumstances.

One thing is absolutely certain—LeeAnn should look into the matter. It is in the best interest of her children to ask as many questions and to raise as many issues as possible.

Jackie's support agreement contained no provision for private school tuition. But she knew for a fact that her ex-husband had gotten a great promotion and a huge raise. Now he could easily afford the tuition. And Jackie was certain that her youngest child would benefit from private school.

Jackie could definitely go to court and request a upward

modification of her child-support award, assuming this change would be in her child's best interest. Whether Jackie would be successful is largely dependent on the law in her state and on whether there is any history of private school for the child.

WHAT IS "A CHANGE OF CIRCUMSTANCES"?

Cheryl, who got a divorce from her prominent radiologist husband five years ago, came to her attorney with a list of her latest support requirements. Her children should have a horse, she stated, and a barn on the property to house it. When her attorney questioned the necessity of the horse, Cheryl said, "You may consider it frivolous, but it fits in perfectly with our lifestyle." She explained that her children were used to pretty much having everything they wanted. "They have been through a real loss," Cheryl reasoned. "This isn't the time for them to start learning to do without."

Courts do look at a family's past lifestyle and take it into account. But there has to be a balance. Some women come to their attorneys with their expectations far too high. There are very few fathers who wouldn't balk at providing and maintaining a horse and paying to have a barn constructed. Also, some mothers simply are out of touch with the limitations of the new lifestyle they have to assume, sometimes because of the divorce and sometimes because of other life events. Some people may be trying to control or seek revenge against an ex through economics. A change of lifestyle caused by a divorce is not a change of circumstances.

A man came to see Nancy about having his support modified. He had been a prosperous movie producer, but had lost that position. His income plummeted overnight to where he was almost bankrupt. His ex-wife, however, was still buying caviar with her children's support money.

"Why not?" she argued. "It is the lifestyle to which I have become accustomed."

She didn't seem able to understand that if she and her husband had still been married, their lifestyle would have gone down drastically. The same would have to happen since they were apart.

We also see this need for downward modification when a parent retires. Since people are having children at older ages, this is happening more and more often. Intact families have to adjust, and so do families which are no longer intact. For the latter, part of the adjustment may show up in reduced child support.

So just what does and does not constitute a change of circumstances? Basically, there must be something that has changed since the original support order was put into effect. It is what we in legal circles know as the concept of ESTOPPEL: You are not allowed to go back and do something that was not originally done. If you did not mention a matter in the first place even though you knew about it, you cannot go back and pick it up later. With few exceptions, if you didn't bring up an issue the first time around, forget it.

Here is an actual example: Even though a father knew his children's mother was a lesbian, he signed an agreement to share custody with her and agreed to have the children live with her. When she decided to move out of state and take the children with her, he filed an action to modify the agreement and change custody. His reason? He insisted that the children should not be exposed to his ex-wife's lesbian lifestyle. The judge refused to allow him to make that argument, however, because this was something he knew all along.

Some of the situations that might be considered a change of circumstance are:

▼ The paying parent goes on disability
▼ The paying parent retires
▼ The paying parent loses his job, or his income is greatly reduced
▼ A child becomes very ill or disabled
▼ A new medical, emotional, or mental diagnosis is made
▼ A child takes longer than expected to finish high school
▼ There are changes in health or life insurance coverage,

either for better or for worse
- ▼ There is a rise in support costs as a child grows older (usually coupled with an increased ability to pay)
- ▼ There are changes that substantially affect either parent's taxes
- ▼ The paying parent gets a new job, or his income increases

Some changes in circumstances do not fit into any category. For instance, in Colorado, a father got a great financial boost when he unexpectedly inherited a nice amount of money. When his children's mother demanded a modification to increase the amount he was paying for child support, the father cried, "No fair!" Since the money wasn't considered income for state or federal income tax purposes, he argued, it shouldn't be considered income for calculating child support either.

The court disagreed. It ruled that any income was fair game for child-support purposes. In addition, since the father had used his inheritance to pay off a lot of debts, he now had a larger amount of money available to him each month. "Pay up," the court ordered.

The unhappy father appealed, but in 1992, the Colorado Appellate Court upheld the ruling (in re. *Marriage of Armstrong*, 1992).

Don't rule out unusual circumstances as a reason for possible modification.

A TEMPORARY CHANGE

What if the person who is paying the support becomes temporarily unable to work—say he had a heart attack or was injured in an automobile accident? Can that be considered a change of circumstances?

Not usually. Modification assumes a permanent change. Temporary changes are difficult to discuss because they vary greatly, not only state to state, but also county to county and judge to judge.

"This problem is especially tough when the economy is poor," Nancy says. "There are so many temporary workers who are technically in contempt of court. And the Child Support Enforcement Agency is not supposed to represent them because it's not a permanent change of circumstance. They can't afford to hire lawyers, and they figure, 'Why should I get one anyway? This is only temporary.'"

Some areas of the country are especially prone to such temporary changes because they depend on seasonal jobs, such as fishing in south Florida and farm work in the central California valley.

In a recent case in Alaska, a father who had worked as a commercial fisherman for several years quit his job. "I'm burned out," he said. "I'm going to go back to school. I'll work while I'm in school, but I will only be earning minimum wage." His ex-wife was not pleased with his decision, and she took him to court. The court, agreeing with the mother, decided to base the father's child-support obligation on his income as a fisherman, averaging his earnings for the three previous years.

The father appealed. "That locks me into working indefinitely as a commercial fisherman," he argued.

In the end, the judgment was upheld. When a person works in an industry where employment and income are erratic, it ruled, it is appropriate to base child support on an average of past income. When the reduced income is voluntary and temporary, the paying parent alone has to bear the results of his reduced income (*Pugil v. Cogar*, 1991).

Most courts would agree.

MODIFYING THE SUPPORT ORDER

It's not enough to go to court and say, "He is earning more money now," or "My child's medical expenses have really increased." You must be able to prove it. The more substantiating information you are able to provide, the better. This is why it is so important that you keep receipts and accurate records.

Again, a modification is not automatic. If your ex is seeking the modification on the grounds that his monthly expenses have gone up, and it turns out that he has bought a new, larger house and is making bigger monthly payments on it, it is unlikely that a judge will agree with his reasoning. If you are seeking the modification because your child would benefit from private school, it just may be that your ex truly doesn't have any more money to contribute. The judge would rule against you as well.

Modification may be ordered, or it may be denied.

Whatever the reason for the modification request, you can be sure that the court will examine it carefully. And with good reason. Consider Sheila's situation.

Sheila requested an upward modification in the child support ordered for her and Dan's four children. "Dan owns his own business, and it's doing extremely well," Sheila said.

"Not at all," Dan argued, and to prove his point he brought in the company books. Sure enough, they showed that after all the expenses had been subtracted, there was little profit left.

But on closer examination, the court discovered that Dan had done some very creative bookkeeping. No wonder the bottom line profits were so low. While Dan and his new wife had no family automobile, the company had two that were driven exclusively by—guess who—Dan and his wife. There were expensive business trips to ski resorts in the winter and lovely vacation spots in the summer. And, since he and his new wife were the only two big-wigs in the company, who do you suppose went on these business trips? Right again. Dan and his wife. Speaking of his wife, she had a huge paycheck issued to her each month from their business. The company also paid for their housekeeper, their lawn service, their auto fuel—just about everything.

The judge was not impressed. He said, "I don't know about all the loans and arrangements I see referred to in your books, and I don't understand a lot of your notations, but I am no fool. Modification granted."

This trick is not only one of the well-to-do. "Creative" bookkeeping is common among the self-employed. One plumber claimed he earned less than minimum wage, and he had the books to prove it. A little investigation turned up the reason—he had only one bank account that served both his business and his personal finances. Therefore he paid everything through his business—groceries, clothes, rent, utilities, car payment. So when he came to the end of the month, he had only about $200 to his name. "That," he told the judge, "is my monthly income—$200."

Fortunately, courts are not easily fooled. Neither are mediators who are trained to point out the realities of the situation in a non-defensive way.

PUSHING THE LIMITS

Brett was a brilliant boy and his mother, Judy, was convinced he was being terribly damaged by his school experience. As he became increasingly bored, he developed into more and more of a troublemaker. "He is so disruptive, we may have to remove him from his regular class," Brett's teacher warned his mother. "He desperately needs to be in a special school that can challenge him and develop his tremendous abilities."

Judy begged Brett's father to help her fund the special school that was recommended to them. "There is no way I can afford it," she said. "But I know you can."

"Public school was good enough for me, and it is good enough for my son," Brett's father stated. "Case closed."

When there seems no way to get the modification, yet you feel it is vital to your child's well-being, what should you do? Stick with it and pull in all the help you can rally. Judy can call on experts to back up her claim about the school's detrimental effect on Brett. She can bring in his teacher to tell what is happening to the boy. She can bring in someone from the alternative school who can spell out the unique opportunities they offer a child like Brett. A private psychologist would probably also help, although that can be quite expensive.

Decide how important the issue is to you. If it's important enough, keep on pushing.

WHO CAN MODIFY?

Either parent can seek modification of a child-support order. As we have seen, it may be approved by the court, or it may be turned down.

A father in Kansas did not get the downward adjustment he wanted. "I'm going to law school soon," he said, "so I'll be earning only about half as much money as before." The court ruled no deal. The mother hadn't even had a chance to get her undergraduate degree yet, they said. Give her a turn (in re. *Marriage of McNeeley*, 1991).

On the other hand, a mother in Alabama did get the modification she asked for. "I've had to go deeply into debt because my ex-husband declared bankruptcy," she told the court. "I have to have more money to pay those debts off." The court agreed. Her debts were affecting the welfare of her children, and the father was able to pay (*Holliday v. Holliday*, 1991).

Who can modify? Anyone who has an acceptable argument and can prove it.

WHO PAYS FOR THE MODIFICATION?

There is no doubt but what the cost of getting a modification can be high. "As a lawyer, I have to say that modifications are the toughest thing to deal with," Nancy says. "People have a mindset that reasons: 'I paid someone to do this once, and he had to handle the whole divorce. This is just a little modification, so it shouldn't cost much at all.' The reality is that the 'little modification' is likely going to take just as much time and effort in order to determine which changes can and should be made. Many people are absolutely shocked when they get the bill from the attorney."

You may or may not have to pay that bill. The judge may order your ex-spouse to pay it. Or he may order you to pay. Or he may order the two of you to each pay half. If the responsible custodial parent brings up a specific point that pulls at the judge's tough old heart strings, he may decide, "Of course she should have that." He might order the modification, then order the father to pay the attorney fees as well.

On the other hand, he might say, "This lady is being unreasonable. She can pay her own bills." Or he might say, "She is being totally reasonable, but, hey, I'm going to have them split the bills."

Since there is no way of knowing which way it will go, be on the safe side and approach the courtroom prepared to pay your own bills. If you have to, you will be ready. If you don't, it will be a wonderful surprise.

IS IT WORTH THE FIGHT?

You may be asking if it is worth the effort. Maybe and maybe not. It all depends. The thing to keep firmly in mind throughout the struggle is that the child-support system is intended to focus on the child's needs rather than on the parent's interests. It is easy to lose sight of this fact. If your battle is being waged for the purpose of seeing your ex punished and thrown in jail, then no, it isn't worth it.

What is your aim in the battle? One woman really wanted her son to have some extras she couldn't provide for him. She consulted the boy's father, but he did not share her vision. "He doesn't need all that," the father said. "If you can earn extra and pay for it, fine. But I am maxed out, and I really don't think it's important."

Now the battle lines are drawn. It is important to her, but it is not important to her child's father. If she gives up, her child will do without. If she fights tooth and nail—which she likely would have to do—there is a good likelihood that she will make an enemy out of her ex.

"So many times we see people who have been getting along just fine until the custodial parent comes to see us because the support check was late or because the children needed something that wasn't included in the support agreement," Ana says. "Then the other parent comes in all upset. 'Why didn't she just call me?' he will ask. 'Why didn't we sit down and talk about it?'

The result is a ruined parenting relationship."

"Things are finally on an even keel," one woman said after fighting with her ex-husband for years. "We both have been trying to get along for the sake of the kids. I would rather do without something than to take him back to court and start the old battles going again."

She is a wise parent to be determining what is and what is not worth fighting for. We advise every client to do the same.

Whether or not a matter is worth the fight largely depends upon what impact it will have on your child. If you literally cannot afford to put food on the table, it is worth it to fight. If your child has a bad dental problem that is affecting his sense of his own worth, it is worth it to fight. If it is a matter of how things look to others, of comparing your situation with what the neighbor across the fence tells you it should be, of extra niceties that would strain your ex-spouse's bank account, or if the emotional stress involved would outweigh the gain, then no, it isn't worth it.

It is important to consider your parenting relationship with your ex. If you are able to cooperate when you need to, if you are both actively working toward your child's good, if your ex is making a real effort to be a good parent, that relationship is likely pretty good. It probably isn't worth sacrificing it to gain a little extra money or other benefits.

Are your children teenagers? If they are nearing the age when they will be out on their own, it probably isn't worth the time and hassle—in addition to the strained relationship—to get support when it will end in a year or two anyway.

If the amount of money your child will get from the modification hardly covers what you will have to spend to get it, it isn't worth it.

Part of wisdom is knowing when to fight and when to quit. If you battle beyond the point of good reason, you may well end up paying for it in therapy.

We have had far too many opportunities to see the destructive results of a battle carried too far. Some people will tell their children, "If your mother comes to your wedding, you can count me out. I won't be there!" or "If you are invit-ing your father to your graduation, don't bother to send me an invitation. I won't be there."

Nancy recalls, "I once had a parent tell me, 'My ex-hus-band and I have a horrible relationship. We can't even go to the hospital at the same time to see our new grandchild.'"

How very, very sad. Whatever their battle, it was not worth it.

On the other hand, some battles are worth fighting to the bitter end because they can have such a far-reaching effect on the child. The courts agree. While judges are well aware of the fact that people's lives change, and they understand that a change of circumstances justifies a reconsideration of the pre-vious court orders, they also know this most important of con-siderations: The deciding factors as to what is and what is not worth the battle is the answer to the question, "Would this change be in your child's best interests?"

CHAPTER NINE
▼ ▼

But a Court Order Won't Pay My Bills!

"RUDY PAYS WHAT HE wants to pay, when he wants to pay it," Sandra said of her ex-husband and the father of her four children. "Most of the time he doesn't want to pay at all."

Sandra has plenty of company. In a presentation at the 1993 American Bar Association Annual Meeting, Diane Dobson of the Washington, D.C.–based Women's Legal Defense Fund stated that in 81 percent of the cases handled by state child-support agencies, no support is collected.

The situation has not been showing much improvement, either. According to a report prepared by the Children's Defense Fund, in 1983 just 14.7 percent of the child-support funds due were collected. Nine years later, in 1992, the collections had risen only slightly, to 18.7 percent.

We can say from personal experience that one of the most frustrating tasks family law professionals face is representing a client whose former spouse does not pay child support even though he can well afford to do so.

"A court order is fine, but what good is it if it isn't enforced?" Sandra asked.

Absolutely none. And you should be aware that the court does not automatically enforce its child-support orders. If your child's other parent is not complying with the support order, nothing will be done until you step forward and take action.

That's the bad news. The good news is that there are a number of legal remedies available to you.

ENFORCING THE SUPPORT ORDER

If you are not receiving your court-ordered child support, there are four options open to you.

1. *You can get a local attorney.* This option is an expensive one, and in many cases there is not a great deal we lawyers can do to help you. If your ex-spouse works for a company, we do have the option of applying for an income deduction order so that the payments will be taken out of his paycheck. As we have seen, this is a lot harder if the parent is self-employed or retired. It is impossible if we cannot find him.

2. *You can retain an attorney where the other parent lives.* If he has moved out of town or left the state, your local attorney may not be able to do much for you. It can be quite expensive to hire an out-of-town lawyer, usually in addition to your local lawyer. If your ex is in another state, any support you're awarded might take a while to get to you. But the biggest disadvantage of this option is that you might well end up in litigation hundreds or even thousands of miles away from home.

3. *You can go to your local social services agency.* As with establishing child support, for a small fee a caseworker and state or government contract attorney will handle your case. Again, the drawback is that family courts do not have the resources to handle the ever-growing number of child-support cases that need to be enforced. As Ana points out, government agencies are under-funded and under-staffed. Sandy Simons, division chief of Santa Barbara, California, County District Attorney's Family Support Division, said, "You can't run out the door on every lead when you have less than

thirty people to cover 25,000 family-support cases."

4. *You can engage the services of a private collection agency*. Private investigators and agencies have joined the family-support collection business all across the U.S. In order to qualify for such a service, you must have a valid court order, your child support must be at least thirty days past due, and you must not have assigned your child-support rights to the state.

These collection agencies generally charge a small up-front fee—$25 or so—then they work on a contingency basis, keeping a percentage of what they collect for you. This means they get paid only if they collect your support money. But the percentage they keep can run as high as 40 percent!

If you decide to go this route, we beg you to be *very careful*. There are few government controls on these agencies, and you can get into real problems. In many states, they do not even have to be licensed in order to operate.

As you can see, each option has advantages, but each also has disadvantages. Before you decide which option is best for you, carefully weigh the pros and cons of each. Your next step may be to consult a lawyer.

"I have no idea what to look for in a lawyer," Sandra said.

WHAT YOU WANT IN AN ATTORNEY

We talked in chapter 4 about how to go about choosing an attorney. Here we must emphasize again the importance of looking for a lawyer who specializes in the field of enforcing child support. This is important because laws, regulations, and acceptable procedures are complicated and constantly changing. This is no time to engage an attorney who has little experience with the child-support enforcement system in your state, or whose experience is so old that for all practical purposes it is out of date.

FINDING AN AGENCY

A network of agencies with eighteen offices in California, Arizona, and Oregon offers an example of what a private collection agency can do for frustrated custodial parents. "We charge nothing until money is collected," one of the investigators states. "When money is received, we take 25 percent of any arrearage collected. Our clients think it is a fair percentage. Seventy-five percent of something is better than 100 percent of nothing!"

Jennifer is one of their satisfied clients. Her ex had disappeared, and she had spent several frustrating months dealing with the district attorney's office. "They couldn't find Doug," she said. "They just have too many cases to spend much time pursuing someone who doesn't want to be found."

When her ex had fallen $1,300 behind in support and she was getting no closer to locating him, Jennifer contacted the agency. Using a check Doug had sent his child for a birthday, the investigator tracked him to North Carolina. The investigator telephoned Doug and warned him that they would be serving him with a summons unless he paid up and kept his payments current. That's all it took. Since then, Doug has sent his checks monthly to the agency, and the agency has forwarded them to Jennifer.

"This warning works about 20 percent of the time," the investigator said. "The rest of the time we have to hire an attorney and take things to court." His clients must cover the attorney's fees.

Not all private collection agencies are able to collect past-due child support effectively. Before you engage any agency, ask yourself these questions:

▼ *Is this agency affiliated with any national organizations, such as the American Child Support Collection Association?* Such an association would afford the agency some degree of professionalism. One agency we contacted said, "We don't have a license or group affiliations. Too much red tape and too many papers to fill out." We would take any response like that as a red flag of warning!

▼ *Are you able to meet with the person who will actually be handling your case?* Talking with him will give you an idea of the agency's professionalism and what the investigator will be like to work with.

▼ *How stable is the agency?* While you may not be able to ask this directly, you can get a good idea by asking such questions as: How long has the agency been in business? How long has it been at this location? How many investigators are on staff? What is the agency's collection record?

▼ *What type of child-support enforcement training have the investigators in this agency had?* It would be wise also to ask how long the agency has been in the child-support collection business.

▼ *What procedures and tactics will the agency use?* Ask, too, if you will be kept informed on what they are doing. It is also important for you to know what say you will have in whether or not to pursue legal actions or to accept settlements.

▼ *May I have references?* Some will not want to provide references because of client confidentiality, but it certainly doesn't hurt to ask.

If you decide to go with the agency, they will ask you to sign a contract. Give yourself plenty of time to read it carefully. Be sure you agree with the percentage you will be charged. Paying 25 percent in fees to receive whatever is in arrearage may be reasonable; 35 or 40 percent is not. Be sure that the money will be paid to you as it is collected rather than being saved for a lump sum. Also be careful that the amount you pay for the initial fee is no more than twenty-five or thirty dollars.

Understand from the beginning that engaging a collection agency will not assure success. Although a professional, experienced agency should have a collection rate of 60 percent or better, there are no guarantees. If an agency makes promises, beware.

Basically, you can look for the same things in a child-support collection agency as you look for in an attorney: experience, stability, and a good rate of success.

GOVERNMENT ENFORCEMENT

Several federal laws have been enacted to enforce child-support judgments. Besides Title IV-D of the Social Security Act, you can get help through the provisions of the Revised Uniform Reciprocal Enforcement of Support Act (RURESA), the Family Support Act of 1988 (FSA), and the Uniform Interstate-Family Support Act (UIFSA). The good thing about the government agencies is that they have real legal clout behind them. They can do things private groups or individuals are not allowed to do—or are not capable of doing. They can arrange to have the overdue support withheld from the ex-spouse's paycheck, they can intercept state and federal tax refunds, they can intercept unemployment compensation, and they can place liens on a parent's personal property.

To start an action under Title IV-D, a parent only needs to fill out an application and pay a modest fee. UIFSA will be in effect in all states by January 1, 1996. Any state that fails to comply with its provisions will no longer be eligible for federal funds.

Let's take a closer look at some of these enforcement tactics.

One: Garnished Wages

In a wage garnishment, an employer is instructed to withhold a specified amount from an employee's wages, then to send a check for that amount to a person designated by the court. It has been proved an extremely successful way to collect child-support payments. The money comes regularly and on time, a record is kept of the payments, and no one has to press or be hassled about it.

Most states allow a delinquent parent's wages to be withheld to pay his child-support debt. There are, however, some states that will not garnish wages. Also, there are specific limits to some state organizations like municipalities. Some states do not allow garnishments over a certain percent. Veterans' benefits and medical disability may be treated specially. These are things to discuss with your attorney or agency.

You can find out how your state handles wage garnishments by checking with your local child-support enforcement office or by looking it up in your state statutes under "wage garnishments," "wage assignments," or "income deduction orders."

Two: Income Deductions
Included in the 1984 Child Support Enforcement Amendments is a requirement that all states enact statutes that provide for mandatory income withholding. This alternative to wage garnishment has been used for some time and is quite effective.

Income deduction, also known as wage assignment or income withholding, differs from wage garnishment in that it applies not only to overdue support, but also to the regular monthly support payments. This is an especially good arrangement for a parent who is delinquent with his payments, because when the debt is paid back, the income deduction automatically keeps him up to date from then on.

Do keep in mind that the laws vary from state to state, and also that changes are continually being made in those laws. In Nevada, for instance, wage assignments are currently not made unless the paying parent requests it, while in Wisconsin, it is now required whenever a support order is given.

Some states use income deductions only when a parent has fallen behind in his child-support payments. In New Hampshire, all child-support orders include a provision that allows income to be withheld as soon as a parent has fallen one month behind in his payments.

If your ex has been with the same employer for some time and there is no reason to think he will be changing jobs, then income withholding can be an excellent solution. As long as he stays with that employer, you will get the support money.

Depending on the state you live in, if he changes jobs you may have to go back to court to get a new order that would then be served on the new employer. In others, a certified copy of the original order would be sent on to the next employer.

"When my ex told me she was going to ask for an income deduction, I was really upset," Ben said. "What are people going to think? It's crazy, because I always pay on time. She says it is the best way to go, but I say it is the best way to damage my career. People will think I'm an undependable jerk who won't support his kids."

"We do hear this complaint, but it doesn't make much sense," Nancy says. "Income deductions are accepted just about everywhere in this country. These have recently been expanded by federal law to include health insurance deductions. Either the objection is just an excuse, or the person is uneducated as to the realities of today."

Three: Tax Intercept

Both the states and the federal government also have tax intercept programs whereby tax refunds can be withheld from parents who are not meeting their child-support commitments. In 1990 alone, 800,000 people used the tax intercept program to collect $509 million. This very successful program requires no additional court hearing after the court finds that an arrearage is owed.

To find out more about these programs, call your local child-support agency.

Four: Contempt Action

Since Rudy was self-employed as a carpenter, and since he had no tax refund due him, none of these options was of much help to Sandra. "I'll have to take him to court," she finally said. "I have no other choice."

This is exactly what most people faced with having to enforce child-support payments end up doing. In fact, it is what most attorneys advise. Although each state has its own procedure, and the courts have their own rules, contempt actions basically follow the same format as Sandra's contempt action against Rudy.

In order for Sandra to prove contempt, the following four things had to be true: (1) There was a child-support order, (2) Rudy knew about the order, (3) he did not comply with the order, and (4) even though he was able to pay, he would not.

Once the conditions were established, the judge listened to what Sandra had to say ("He owes the money, and we can't pay our bills without it") and what Rudy had to say ("It's too much; I've got to have some life for myself"). The only justifiable defense Rudy could have given was that he was unable to pay.

"He works," Sandra reasoned. "Of course he can pay."

Generally, that reasoning is right. Even if Rudy were not working, most courts agree that if a parent is healthy and capable of holding down a job, it is his obligation to find work and pay his court-ordered support. (This is also true of a mother who has been ordered to pay child support, by the way.)

When a parent is unemployed or voluntarily underemployed (versus being unable to pay because he is disabled by an accident or illness) the court may still impute his income into the guideline, but it may impute only if the parent has the *actual* ability to earn that amount. If a parent loses his job and has no ability to get another one at the same pay rate, the court cannot impute at the prior rate. Likewise, if the parent is merely between jobs, it would not be fair to calculate his income at zero. The court has the responsibility of imputing a fair income to that parent. This is very subjective and since each party must present its strongest case at the hearing, it is usually a heavily argued issue.

Once the court establishes the amount of support, regardless of whether or not income was imputed, the parent must pay or risk being found in contempt of the court order. If the court finds that the parent failed to pay during a period of time when he did *not* have the ability to pay, the court can't find him in contempt of court. This does not mean that the arrearages are forgiven, just that he is not in contempt and therefore can't be incarcerated. If child support was established based on imputed income and the good faith belief that the parent had the ability to earn the imputed amount, and it is later clear that there has been a change (job market, demand, disability, etc.) that parent can seek a modification of the support order.

"Let Sandra prove I can pay!" Rudy challenged.

She doesn't have to. If he cannot pay, it is up to him to prove it to the court.

It didn't take the judge long to make his decision—Rudy owed the money and he *would pay*. The judge also determined the amount of overdue support money Rudy owed.

What will happen now? That depends. If the judge finds that Rudy has enough assets available to purge, he may send Rudy to jail until he pays a specified amount. If the judge finds he doesn't have enough assets, he still can find Rudy in contempt, but he will order Rudy to make an additional monthly payment to go toward the arrears.

You may say, "I don't want my ex to get off that easy."

Actually initial leniency makes good sense. If the delinquent parent is sent to jail, he cannot go to work, and this may risk his job. If he sees that you are not about to throw your hands in the air helplessly and sit still and let him get by without making his payments, there is a good chance he will be jarred into more responsible action. If you show him you are prepared to do whatever you have to do to get that child-support judgment honored, he just may manage to find the money he owes.

LOCATING A DELINQUENT PARENT

"None of this applies to me," Shelly said. "When Joel got tired of paying, he just disappeared. I mean, he's gone. There is nothing I can do."

Don't give up too easily. Even though your ex has moved away, even though you have no idea where he has gone, there is help for you. Start by contacting the local social services agency and asking about the Parent Locator Service (PLS). Also coming out of the Federal Child Support Enforcement Act, PLS serves as a clearing house for information on child-support evaders whose whereabouts are unknown. Some states also have parent locator services that can help locate delinquent parents when the state they are in is known.

When Shelly makes an appointment with a caseworker to make use of PLS, she should bring Joel's social security number. By linking it up by computer with information they have from the Department of Labor, they may be able to find out where Joel is working. With a work address, they will be able to serve a subpoena right on his job. Shelly should also bring along a picture of Joel and any other information she can think of that will help the process servers identify him.

Joel was finally located—2,000 miles away.

"Well, I guess that's that," Shelly sighed. "I sure can't pursue the matter now. He was determined to get away, and it looks like he made it."

URESA

It's amazing the extent to which some parents will go to keep from paying their court-ordered child support. A southern California surgeon who owned a million-dollar home and earned $12,000 a month in a thriving medical practice is now a fugitive. Investigators say he owes $250,000 in unpaid child support.

When parents are this determined to avoid their responsibilities, it can be hard to track them down. However, with today's computer networks, the task is much easier than it was just a few years ago. But finding deadbeats is only the beginning. They still have to be brought to court. One program that has made it easier to prosecute out-of-state cases is the Uniform Reciprocal Enforcement of Support Act (URESA). This legislation is recognized in all fifty states. A handful of states have now adopted the Uniform Interstate Family Support Act (UIFSA). This updated law, although similar to URESA, provides that an order of support does not change if the noncustodial parent moves to another state. Depending on where the absent parent lives, either URESA or UIFSA will apply. If your ex has moved, check into this to see whether your child-support amount will change.

Under URESA, Shelly can file a petition in her own state that will result in a hearing in the state in which Joel now lives. She will not even have to attend that hearing.

Scott was another parent who was helped by URESA. Hannah, his ex-wife, didn't go anywhere, but Scott did. After their divorce, he left Ohio and moved back to West Virginia to live with his family. When Hannah stopped paying child support, Scott said, "I guess I'll have to get an attorney."

That was one option open to him. But if Scott chooses to use a private attorney, he may have to retain an attorney in Ohio as well as one in West Virginia. Besides paying two attorneys, he would have to pay to travel to Ohio for the hearing. And of course things could go wrong—a postponement of the hearing, expensive long-distance telephone calls to his attorney, Hannah failing to appear at the hearing, and so forth.

Fortunately Scott was told about URESA. When he went to his initial appointment, he brought along Hannah's social security number and a copy of the child-support order to show that she was indeed under court order to pay. Since he knew where Hannah worked, he was also able to provide the name of her employer. Under URESA, Scott was able to file the petition in West Virginia and the papers were sent on to Ohio, which held jurisdiction over the child-support judgment.

Had Ohio been unable to find Hannah, it would have informed West Virginia. Since she was quickly located, however, the matter proceeded just as if it were any other civil case: A hearing was scheduled, and Hannah was ordered to pay up.

Had Hannah disagreed about her obligation, she would have been given the right to argue her case. But since she didn't fight, a court order was issued. The hearing was held, and Scott never had to leave West Virginia.

Since Hannah lived in Ohio and Ohio is where the original order was established, the court has the power to enforce the judgment. It was different for Joel. Since he had moved out of the state where the order was issued, his hearing established jurisdiction over him in the state where he now lived. That way, that court had the power to enforce the order.

Scott's support remained at the level it had originally been set. Not so with Joel.

"People think the support is going to be the same amount as it was in the state where the original judgment was made, but that is not necessarily true," Ana says. "What happens under URESA is that a new support judgment is ordered in the other state. Basically, the whole thing starts all over again."

Because state guidelines are not uniform, the same facts will often bring about different awards in different states. Joel was pleased to find that his new support order reduced the amount he was to pay by $25 each week. "Wow," he said as he walked out of the courtroom. "This was my lucky day."

Maybe and maybe not. That lesser amount does not stop the clock from ticking in the original state. Each month, Joel will still be racking up a $25 debt out there. Technically that first state could sometime bring an action for the arrearages, although this is unlikely. Probably nothing will happen unless he decides to come back to his home state, something he may well want to do down the line.

"The thing to understand is that the debt is not erased," Ana points out. "In fact, it can be getting larger by incurring interest."

Jonathan found that out the hard way. He and Linda, his ex-wife, owned a sprawling ranch-style house in Arizona. When they divorced, they agreed that Linda would live in the house until their youngest child, a five-year-old, turned eighteen. Then, at that time, the house would be sold and they would split the profit. The problem began when Jonathan, like Joel, moved to another state and got a judgment for a lower support settlement there. Each month for the next thirteen years, Jonathan's support arrearage in Arizona kept going up and up. When the children reached majority, his debt was over $4000.

Linda got a judgment against Jonathan's half interest in the house. To Jonathan's dismay, when Linda put his interest in the house up for auction, he found that no one was interested in bidding on half interest in a house with someone they didn't even know. In the end, Linda ended up with the entire equity of their house.

CRACKING DOWN

In California, a delinquent parent was outraged when his three-year-old Harley-Davidson motorcycle was seized and sold at auction to the highest bidder. The money was used to pay the $30,000 child-support debt he had racked up. "Instead of paying child support, he's buying toys," said a criminal investigator for the district attorney's family support division.

In cities all over the U.S., officials are asking the public to help find the deadbeats. One city issues an annual "Ten Most Wanted" poster. It carries mug shots of ten men who have skipped out on their child-support payments. Other cities display their most wanted on television, on milk cartons, or publish their names and pictures in the newspaper.

In Florida, a man ran up a $106,000 bill for child support and legal costs during the fifteen years it took his former wife to track him down after he left the family in Washington. When she found him—he had a new name, a third wife, and a son—he was jailed for thirty days and ordered to pay $100 per week in back child support.

Seizures of private property are rare in child-support cases. Usually it is an action of last resort. So are "most wanted" posters and lists of names and television exposure. But these tactics are happening with more and more frequency.

For many years, parents whose ex-spouses would not pay had no choice but to struggle on alone, turn to relatives and friends, or fall back on the government for support. There were few agencies to help them, and the public heard little about their plight.

No longer. Now lawmakers—and the public as a whole—are getting fed up with deadbeat parents who cannot be bothered to support their children.

Don't give up on getting your order enforced. Help is available.

▼ ▼

Feeling Good About Yourself

REBECCA WAS USED to living the good life. When she married Jeff, he had just taken over his father's successful construction company. By the time Nathan and Kim came along, Jeff was earning good money. Rebecca enjoyed the best of comfortable living—lovely clothes, an exquisite home, a full-time maid, trips to Europe.

All that changed when Jeff's penchant toward using alcohol to relax developed into full-blown alcoholism. As his drinking grew worse, Jeff became involved with another woman and his business fell apart.

Rebecca stood by helplessly. Her blood pressure soared, and she began to experience heart problems. Then other health troubles followed. "You need a hysterectomy," her doctor told her. Rebecca didn't even consider it. With no health insurance and little money coming in, she knew there was no way she could afford an operation.

Yet through it all, Rebecca refused to grow bitter. "Even though things look bad, I just know our family will come through this," she insisted.

Then came the day when Jeff announced that he was leaving Rebecca to start a new life with his girlfriend. Confused and hurt, Rebecca turned to her children for comfort. She was not prepared for their response.

"Dad's gone, and now we have nothing," Nathan said angrily. "Thanks a lot!"

"We never do anything fun anymore," added Kim, "and it's all your fault."

Both kids agreed: Obviously Mom had done something terribly wrong. Surely the disasters that had befallen their family were her fault.

Rebecca had little time to mourn her loss. She had to have some money coming in. It did no good to press Jeff. He had nothing himself, and anyway Nathan had already turned eighteen and Kim would be a minor only for another year and a half, so it was hardly worth fighting for child support. Yet what could Rebecca do? She had never held down a job. Now well into her forties, it made no sense to start back to school. It would take too long. She had rent to pay and food to buy right now.

"Get a job, any job," her friends advised.

Rebecca soon learned that was easier said than done. There is not much available for a forty-six-year-old woman with little education and no employment experience. Her only work credit was housework and mothering. "I have to do what I know," she reasoned. So she started working as a domestic.

Even through all of this, Rebecca refused to give in to self-pity. "God has blessed me with a strong back," she pointed out. "And hard work is good for me."

Today Nathan, who is in college, and Kim, who is anxiously preparing for graduation from high school, are doing fine. Both sometimes help their mother clean houses. When she looks at them she says with definite pride, "They have grown into good, responsible people." She is way too humble to add that it was she who taught them by her example.

With all she has been through, how can Rebecca maintain her positive attitude? She explains it this way: "Long ago I determined that the only way I could live happily is to make up my mind to do the best I can with what I have. I refuse to dwell on what might have been."

Sometimes it is terribly hard to keep a positive attitude—especially when your ex-spouse denounces you as money hungry, and your former in-laws call you selfish and unfair, and people you thought were your friends chide you for being vengeful. It is especially devastating to have your children seem ungrateful for all you have done for them. Such pronouncements can so undermine your self-esteem that you end up feeling guilty and defensive. In time you may even decide that you deserve all those negative descriptions.

When you are feeling your worst, look at your kids and refocus on the purpose behind your efforts: You are working not only for your future, but for the future of your children.

YOU ARE CARING FOR YOUR CHILD

If it feels like your struggle is just a battle of your side against your ex's side, you need to pull back and ask yourself, "Am I losing sight of the purpose here? Am I forgetting what this is all about?" By enforcing the law of the land, you are caring for your child. Your child's welfare is the whole reason for taking the child-support action to court in the first place.

Remind yourself over and over again that your child has the right to the best quality of life you are capable of providing for him. You owe it to him to give him the healthiest, most solid start you possibly can. Throughout your lifetime you will find yourself filling many roles: child, sibling, employee, parent, friend, spouse, and on and on. But of them all, the role that will be your most pivotal and influential will undoubtedly be that of parent. What you do now during the years of your son's childhood will set your little one on a course that will bless him or beset him for the rest of his life. It is your sacred responsibility, as well as your precious privilege, to give your very best performance as you play the role of caring parent.

THE CARING PARENT ROLE

Virginia was one mother who had a great deal of trouble keeping her focus on her child. "I can't stop remembering how much better our life was before the divorce," she said. "Before

I didn't have to be so concerned with money. Now I always feel uncomfortable around my friends. Their clothes are nicer, their homes are more impressive, they take better vacations. I can't help wanting to be like them."

Do you share Virginia's struggle? Somehow we all seem to continually compare ourselves with people who are ahead of us, never with those who are struggling even more than we are. So if you compare, you are always going to feel that you are behind. If you are an ex-wife, the odds are that you really have suffered a setback since your divorce. Statistics show that the man recovers financially five years after the divorce, then he goes on with his life. But it is different for most ex-wives. If a woman doesn't remarry, she probably won't ever be able to build back up to that previous standard of living.

"Well," Virginia added, "all I can say is, the time will come when that man I was married to will get what is coming to him. And I just hope I am around to see it happen."

Poor Virginia. Ex-spouses who pine away demanding justice and plotting revenge and harboring bitterness are piling up misery for themselves. Those negative feelings do absolutely nothing to your ex and his new wife, but that well of bitterness can destroy you, both physically and emotionally. If that happens to you, what kind of a parent will you be able to be?

A caring parent recognizes the concept of forgiveness as the healing balm it is.

"Forgiveness may be for some women," Virginia said, "but you obviously never knew my ex. He was and still is a first-class jerk. My children deserve to know what I put up with from him. They have a right to see him for what he is rather than for the wonderful act he puts on in front of them."

We realize that it is mighty hard for people who are as hurt and angry as Virginia to understand, but constantly running an ex down not only is bad for her children, it also keeps her down. Letting go of that anger and bitterness is a matter of self-preservation.

We talked in chapter 5 about the deep emotional impact

problems surrounding child support thrust onto everyone involved. The best thing you can do right now is step back from your emotions and operate in as realistic and mature a way as you possibly can. If you can accomplish the things you need to accomplish, if you can manage to shoulder the responsibility for your child that is suddenly forced on you, you will come through feeling good about the job you have done. And you will be freed from the guilt of feeling you should have done something differently.

You may be saying, "That's all well and good, but my emotions are too strong. I can't overcome them."

Do the best you can. It is terribly hard, but the price of not doing it is just too high. Giving in to those emotions will allow them to overtake you, and the resulting bitterness and guilt can destroy you.

Nancy recalls a woman she worked with recently whose ex-husband showed up for the mediation session in a chauffeured limousine. As Nancy gathered information on him, she learned that he earned over $200,000 a year.

In a private conversation, the woman told Nancy that she had trouble keeping her mind on the sessions. "The whole time I kept calculating the small percentage of that fortune that was coming to our children, and how much he has left for his own extravagances."

"That woman's feelings were completely natural, a very human response to the situation," Nancy says. "The last thing she needed was for me to pass judgment on her. But after assuring this lady that her emotions were normal, I needed to tell her that the best choice was to acknowledge her feelings, then let them go."

Ana adds, "It is also important to do away with anger. Although anger too is normal and natural, harboring it is harmful for everyone involved. It, too, needs to be acknowledged, dealt with, then set aside."

If you cannot get past the anger, you are going to be seeing things behind every corner. In everything that happens you will say, "Somehow, I know he is doing this to take advantage of me." You must understand that endless suspicions can destroy you. And the pressure suspicions put on children is terribly unfair. We see many situations where a parent warns a child, "We can't do what you are asking. If we do, your father will know we have money and he'll cause us trouble. We must not let him see or know anything about us." A caring parent does not make a co-conspirator of her child.

Playing the role of caring parent goes beyond putting yourself in a healthy state of mind and emotion. That is only the beginning. Once that is done, it is time to reach out and assertively take charge.

TAKING CHARGE

"But there is nothing I can do," Virginia insisted.

Nothing? Rebecca would not settle for that helpless outlook. If you cannot find the job you really want, take a lesser job to keep you going while you continue to look for something better. If you will be getting alimony for a few years, use that time to prepare to support yourself. If you are on government assistance, determine that it will only be a bridge over a difficult time in your life, and begin working now toward becoming independent.

"But I have no job skills," Virginia pointed out.

Then determine to get some. There is no better time than now. Look for classes in local colleges and adult education offerings, seek out training programs, apply for basic jobs that will allow you to work your way up.

"A junior college in this area offers a good program," Ana says. "They take women who are interested in going into the workplace and teach them the things they need to know in order to compete: how to balance a checkbook, how to do simple budgeting and financial planning, how to research job opportunities, how to prepare a résumé, how to act at an interview. They also provide counseling and a support group for women in transition. The classes have been extremely successful in helping women to feel good about themselves and getting them ready to move out into the community."

Check with your local colleges to see what they offer. Don't neglect the extended-education selections. Also watch for training classes offered by corporations, service organizations, and your community.

"Not only will taking charge of your life help you financially and emotionally, it will help you in terms of the presentation of your case to the judge or in expressing yourself in mediation," Nancy adds. "Judges have more respect for individuals who are out there trying to find out what they can do for themselves and how they can get fully involved in life. And your ex needs to hear in mediation what your efforts have been."

IF YOU NEED HELP

"The other day I overheard something that broke my heart," Charlotte said. "My mother asked my eleven-year-old son how he was doing and he told her, 'I feel like a piece of meat. Dad is pulling on one end and Mom is pulling on the other end. I'm tough enough that I don't rip in half, but I always hurt.'"

How tragic. It isn't wise to exclude children from the family's problems, because then they won't learn the skills that will allow them to develop into problem-solvers. On the other hand, it tears children apart to have to hear all the bitterness and anger and recriminations that fly between their parents.

"I try to restrain myself, but the pressure builds and builds until I blow up," Charlotte said. "I try, I really do, but I just cannot control myself. I feel terrible about what I'm doing to my son, but I'm helpless to make any changes."

It never occurred to Charlotte to ask for help. When it was suggested to her, she exclaimed, "Oh, no! I can take care of this by myself."

Like Charlotte, many people resist asking for help because they see that as a sign of weakness. In truth, just the opposite is so. It takes a great deal of courage and strength for a person to say, "This is a problem I cannot solve alone. I need help."

Too often we who are in the position of advising people in difficult situations have to share the blame. By emphasizing only the problems and none of the solutions, we add to their discouragement and sense of helplessness. We have a responsibility to point out the strengths in an individual's situation and to present alternatives for coping with the problems. Yet we are not counselors, and we do not have the time and resources to act as such. In the end, it is up to the woman herself to take charge and seek out a professional who is better equipped to see the situation objectively.

If you are concerned about your own ability to meet your emotional challenges, a counselor or support group can go a long way toward helping you discover ways to make the most of your strengths and to cope with your weaknesses. You may even find that some of those besetting weaknesses can be turned around to where they actually become strengths.

It may be that you are seeing troubling behaviors in your child that concern you. Again, a professional counselor might be the best person to help you determine whether or not your child needs professional attention. A counselor can also be helpful to you by providing direction in how to go about helping your child through this difficult time. Check to see if part of the cost is covered by insurance. If a private counselor is too expensive, consult with the psychologist at your child's school. Or you can contact your local mental-health clinic.

So how do you know if you need professional help to work through troubling issues in your life? Look at the following questions. Any yes answers indicate that you could benefit from talking with a professional counselor. The more yes answers you have, the more important it is.

YES NO

❑   ❑   Do you have trouble communicating with your child? With your ex? With his new spouse?

❑   ❑   Are any members of your family acting in a violent or threatening way toward other family members?

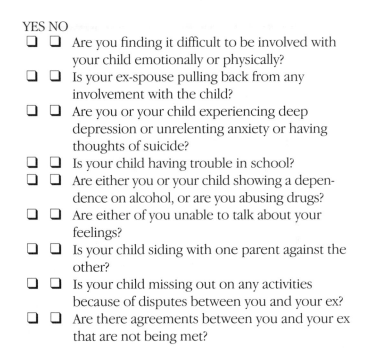

YES NO

❏ ❏ Are you finding it difficult to be involved with your child emotionally or physically?

❏ ❏ Is your ex-spouse pulling back from any involvement with the child?

❏ ❏ Are you or your child experiencing deep depression or unrelenting anxiety or having thoughts of suicide?

❏ ❏ Is your child having trouble in school?

❏ ❏ Are either you or your child showing a dependence on alcohol, or are you abusing drugs?

❏ ❏ Are either of you unable to talk about your feelings?

❏ ❏ Is your child siding with one parent against the other?

❏ ❏ Is your child missing out on any activities because of disputes between you and your ex?

❏ ❏ Are there agreements between you and your ex that are not being met?

"I really don't need any more advice," Charlotte said firmly. "I get more than enough of that from my friends and family."

No doubt. But that advice is not the same as what a counselor provides. Even though loved ones care a great deal, and though they mean well, advice from friends and relatives often ends up making the situation worse. Few of those people are trained counselors. Even if they are, it is very hard for people so close and caring to be objective.

It may be that a patient, listening ear is all you will need. Many times a close friend can provide that—especially if that person can resist the impulse to counsel you when all you want her to do is listen. You might come right out and tell such a person that you are not asking for advice; you find it comforting just to be able to express your fears and anxieties to someone who cares. Trained counselors are masters at listening. Support groups can also be great helps.

Other people find it aids in the healing process to write

their feelings and fears down in a journal or to express them through music or artistic endeavors. Others find great comfort and rejuvenation in prayer and meditation. Discover what works for you, and use it to set you on the road to healing.

"I wouldn't know how to choose a counselor," Charlotte said. "Should I just look in the telephone directory?"

No. There will likely be people listed who have little training, or whose training is badly outdated. It would be better to contact the Family Service Agency in your area or to ask for recommendations from your family doctor, your minister or priest, or people who have used a counselor themselves.

Once you have the name of a potential counselor, go about evaluating her just as you would a lawyer. Ask about her credentials, her training, her experience in helping people in situations similar to yours, and the number of years she has been in practice. Have an initial meeting together so you can see whether or not you would feel comfortable working with her.

One last word: *Don't wait too long to seek help.* Early assistance can often prevent serious, lasting problems from developing.

THE END RESULT IS WELL WORTH THE FIGHT

To be successful in your quest to do the best you possibly can for your child and to come out at the end of the process feeling good about yourself, there is a major requirement: *Take the responsibility.* Don't rely only on your lawyer. Don't rely on an investigator. It will take time and effort to make yourself aware and to become more involved, but look at it as an investment that will pay off handsomely in the end.

No one is arguing that changes don't need to be made in many areas of child support, but until those changes are made, the burden of responsibility for your child rests on your shoulders.

It's never easy to be a parent. All parents make mistakes. But if you maintain a good relationship with your children, and if they feel your love and acceptance, they will move beyond your mistakes and remember your love and caring.

Do you feel like giving up? Don't. Keep on even when you feel you can't do it any more. To succeed in this difficult role in which you have been cast, you will need energy, resourcefulness, and determination. But the good news is that you *can* succeed. If, because of your efforts, your child has a better start in life—a more acceptable standard of living, a better education, the opportunity to spend more time with you—then you have achieved an enormous victory. It will be well worth the fight.

▼ ▼

CHAPTER ELEVEN

Where Does the U.S. Go from Here?

"STIFF YOUR KIDS, star on TV. That's the message of 'Deadbeat Parents,' a new entry in the fall lineup that zooms in on child support scofflaws." So read a recent Associated Press article. It seems that the goal of this show, which made its debut in 1993 in Contra Costa County, California, is to embarrass delinquent parents into paying up. After a brief introduction, viewers are shown pictures and vital statistics of ten deadbeat parents, followed by a telephone number viewers can call if they have any information on the wanted men and women. The list is no respecter of status. Alleged deadbeats have included a stockbroker, a tattoo artist, and a medical doctor.

Actually, this isn't a totally unique idea. Television spots have been broadcast in various areas of California for a while. Several states circulate "most wanted" posters of alleged deadbeat parents.

Both Massachusetts and Florida have made willful nonpayment of child support a felony punishable by up to five years in prison. In Maine, a 1993 law, which allows authorities to take away professional and driver's licenses of parents who don't pay, is persuading deadbeat parents to hand over approximately one million dollars a month.

States are getting serious about the problem of parents who don't pay to support their children.

WHICH STATES ARE SUCCEEDING?

Many states deserve a pat on the back for taking steps both to prosecute deadbeat parents and to assist parents who are left shouldering the entire responsibility of supporting their children. Even more encouraging, new legislation is coming along all the time throughout the United States. To show you what we mean, let's look at several noteworthy pacesetting states and see what they are doing right.

Michigan

When we look at states that are dealing with child support actively and innovatively, Michigan immediately stands out. Its Friends of the Court Program has been singularly successful. The impersonal bureaucratic approach encountered in so many states has been replaced in Michigan by a system that is far less threatening to parents seeking help with child support. A parent can make an appointment to go in and work the support out in an atmosphere that is helpful and encouraging rather than adversarial. Michigan also supports mediation. Since the system has been in place for fifty years, their staff is experienced.

Massachusetts

Massachusetts has computerized its child-support collection method with striking results. Under state law, employers have two weeks to report the names of new employees and any pertinent child-support information. This information is then entered into a state computer, and within twenty-four hours the employer is notified of the amount of money he is to withdraw from that employee's paycheck for child support.

By matching tax records with child-support records, Massachusetts also puts bank liens on the account of any nonpaying parent's account. In just one month, this technique raked in $4.3 million in delinquent child-support payments.

Iowa

Certainly enforcement is a vital part of a successful child-support program, but enforcement alone is not enough. As we have seen, much more needs to be done to improve relations between a child's two parents, starting with communication. The Iowa Access Project is one promising approach. This program offers mediation services to estranged couples.

Florida

In the promising area of mediation, Florida is definitely in the forefront. Besides established training standards for mediators and mediation education programs, Florida has both grievance standards and grievance procedures for them. The program is obviously working, because 70 percent of the cases mediated are resolved by this process. In addition, Florida is in the forefront of child-support collections with laws that allow for automatic liens on real property, lottery intercepts, unemployment compensation deductions, and the suspension of professional and driver's licenses. Income deductions are automatic and mandatory.

More Success

Earlier we mentioned the discouraging statistics on child-support collections. Nationwide in the U.S., collections have grown a mere 4 percent between 1983 and 1992. But some states have done a whole lot better. In those nine years, in New Mexico, North Dakota, and Wyoming collections have increased by approximately 12 percent. West Virginia increased by 14 percent, and Virginia by 15 percent. Missouri climbed by 17 percent, and South Carolina and South Dakota by approximately 18 percent. In Kansas and Montana the increase was 20 percent, and in Hawaii, which posted the largest increase, it was by 21 percent. In Vermont, the rate has increased from a 24.7 percent collection rate to a rate of 40.3 percent, making it the number-one state in the percentage of child-support collections.

Yet even as states demonstrate areas of success, we recognize that there is still a lot to be done.

A MODEL FOR THE FUTURE

Where should we go from here? We would like to suggest twelve points that need to become routine child-support procedures if the U.S. is to see real progress in the percentages paid.

One: Awareness in the Court

Judges who handle child-support cases need to be in touch with the circumstances of single parents who depend on those payments. While this is already the case in some courts, it is unfortunately still the exception. Too many judges today are simply out of touch with the plight of custodial parents. Many judges grew up in intact middle-class families. Their mothers were homemakers who were often waiting to greet their children with cookies and milk when they got home from school.

This Ozzie and Harriet picture is a far cry from the present experience of the general American population, let alone the experience of the crumbling families who every day approach judges' benches across the country pressing for support for their children. Courts of the future need to be presided over by judges well trained in the realities of life as they exist for parents seeking child support.

Two: Specifically Trained Attorneys

Family law has been a bit of a stepchild of the legal profession, especially in the very tradition-oriented law schools. In most law schools, there is very little study in the area of family law, usually not much more than the general principles of divorce law. There is nothing offered on mediation or counseling. A model for the future would include more lawyers sufficiently trained in the area of family law as well as in alternative dispute-resolution processes such as mediation. (It is, after all, one of the fastest growing areas in the law!) Law schools would put more emphasis on this extremely important concentration. They would also do a better job of offering their students clinical situations in which to practice creative thinking as opposed to looking strictly at the letter of the law.

The bottom-line reality is that law schools are primarily funded by the gifts of the alumni, and those alumni are not often practicing family law. Talk show giant Oprah Winfrey has set an impressive precedent by funding five scholarships annually for Loyola Law School in Chicago. Scholarship winners will specialize in issues that assist children, then upon passing the bar will work as child advocate attorneys. In the future, other foundations and law schools should be actively encouraged to provide this sort of funding.

Three: Day Care

"One of the biggest problems faced by custodial parents is a lack of affordable day care," Ana says.

Many girls are having children at a young age, and the majority of these teens do not get the education they need to be competitive in the job market. They have very little chance of ever moving beyond the lowest end of the pay scale.

Some of the proposed reform plans provide free day care for mothers who are in school and are being trained for jobs, but once the education is over, the day care is dropped. What then? Even if a young woman does finish high school, there is little chance she will get a job that will pay her enough to allow her to afford child care. Affordable day care must be available on a permanent basis.

Our model for the future would see custodial mothers trained to provide reliable, affordable day care for other mothers. The job those child-care givers perform would allow other mothers to go out and work. This may require government intervention, but isn't that better than keeping generation after generation on AFDC?

Four: Wage Deductions

Our model for the future would include reforms guaranteeing that newly hired employees who have child-support responsibilities would be quickly set up for income deductions.

The federal government already requires employers to file

a form every three months reporting new employees. Even so, it is estimated that a quarter of the parents who owe child support quit or change jobs before wage withholding ever begins. If wage withholding could be speeded up to ten days, the program would bring in four times the amount in increased child-support collections as it would cost the government to administer the improved version. Unemployed nonpaying parents should be given city and government managed jobs, with the child support taken off the top and sent directly to the custodial parents. Then there is no excuse for not taking responsibility.

Five: Universal Guidelines

As it stands now, every state decides how much child support an absent parent should pay. Even after making adjustments for differences in the cost of living from state to state, child-support awards vary enormously—from $25 a month for a low-income parent in New York to $327 a month for a parent of the same profile in Indiana. Universal guidelines to make the amount of support consistent across the country are badly needed.

Six: Paternity

Mary Jo Bane, currently the top child-support official on the federal level, calls establishing paternity "the area where we most need dramatic improvement." To date, three states—Washington, Delaware, and Virginia—already have innovative programs that allow fathers to be identified right at the hospital.

Mothers should be encouraged to acknowledge paternity at the time the birth certificate is filled out. In the case of fathers who argue or question their paternity, genetic testing should be available at the time of the baby's birth, and it should be available at every hospital across the U.S. If the father can't afford it, the state should pay the tab. To those who complain that this would be too expensive we say, "The cost of the testing is a lot less than the cost of supporting the child until he reaches eighteen!"

Seven: Faster, More Complete Service

The courts are so clogged with stacks of child-support cases that it can take a frustratingly long time for a parent to get her case heard. This process needs to be expedited. One way to do this is to present the cases before hearing officers rather than judges. Hearing officers are already being used in some places—and quite successfully at that. In Florida on a regular basis they preside over massive numbers of hearings. This approach is gaining popularity in several states.

Besides more speedy hearings, people are also asking for more of a full-service approach. "In the future, I think we will see a Wal-Mart–type cluster concept in the area of family law," Nancy says. "People will want to go to one full-service place rather than having to run here and there for the various services they need. More and more, family practice attorneys will be called on to give advice on insurance, financial concerns, psychological concerns, and even to do some counseling in the area of divorce and child support. People can't afford to go to all these specialists. And more and more, they are becoming used to getting the job done in one stop."

At this time ethical rules don't allow attorneys to have such diverse business relationships, so this approach will be a major change in focus. But it is definitely the wave of the future.

Eight: Consistent Reviews

Child-support awards should be reviewed consistently and routinely. This should be done at least once every three years. Things do change—jobs come and go, incomes increase and decrease, insurance policies are started up and they are canceled, children's needs go up and they also go down.

"Often I will have people put a clause in their mediation agreement that they will meet every three years, and both will bring their tax returns along with them," Nancy says. "This saves them from having to go back to hire an attorney to deal with changes."

In our model for the future, reviews would be as normal and routine as renewing a driver's license.

Nine: Payments Through the IRS

Lynn Woolsey, the first welfare mother to serve in Congress, is convinced that the way to protect other parents from becoming victims of deadbeats like she was is to turn the collection of child support over to the Internal Revenue Service. There are various ways in which this could be accomplished, but one approach would be to have a national registry of child-support orders. Employers would be required to withhold payments from an employee's paycheck and forward the money to the IRS. The IRS would in turn send the money to the custodial parent.

"We have to do better for our children," Woolsey insists. Backers of this plan insist it is the only way consistent collection will ever come about.

Ten: Stepparents' Rights and Responsibilities

Across the U.S., more and more people are insisting on additional rights for stepparents. "I have raised my stepson since he was four years old," a stepfather said. "Yet if my wife died, I would have no legal rights to have contact with the boy." Others counter, "Yes, but it is the biological father who pays support year after year. If stepparents get rights, they should also get responsibility. Let them pay support."

In our model for the future, guidelines will include a consideration of stepparents' rights and responsibilities. When a child truly has needs and a stepparent desires rights, it is not unreasonable for the court to look to that stepparent for some support. Yet many factors would need to be considered, such as: Is a biological parent paying child support? Is there life insurance that will protect the child in the event of a parent's death? Who else is contributing to the child's support?

Eleven: Mediation

In areas where mediation has been used, it has proven to be very successful. "If people can walk away from a bad situation feeling that they have had some control over the outcome, that they have won something, they will be more likely to work with each other and to adhere to the judgment," Ana says.

Nancy adds, "When people are in a divorce situation, they tend to be at their worst. Many come in terribly angry, and they get advice from people that feeds their anger. I think mediators have a wonderful opportunity to assist and educate because they are neutral in a positive way. They are also in a position to help people understand the economic decisions that were made."

People don't need to be in the courtroom tearing each other down. Rather than telling people that the way to resolve their problems is to go to court, our model for the future would provide assistance that would encourage them to resolve disputes through negotiation and mediation. These are far better methods for dealing with child-support disagreements.

Nancy says, "Some people come to see me for mediation because they are so frustrated with their spouses that they just have to do something. It is a way to let their spouses know how bad things are getting between them."

"Even though I have very little time to spend with an individual, if I see a glimmer of hope for her marriage, or if I can tell she and her spouse haven't really talked things over, I tell her to go home and talk with him, then to come back a week later," Ana says. "This is so important, because many people think once their spouse gets a summons, he (or she) will straighten up and act like a good husband (or wife). But in fact the summons only makes things worse. I can't provide real mediation—as an attorney I don't have time. But even just the little I can do makes a difference."

Mediated agreements would play a big part in our model for the future. Not only would they save people money and ease hostilities between the two people involved, they would surely preserve some families.

Twelve: Responsibility Taught

The cornerstone of our model for the future is teaching people to accept responsibility. We need to start talking to kids at an early age about what happens when a person parents a child, whether or not that person is married. Young people need to know that with parenthood comes great responsibility. As a society, we need to begin teaching—and modeling—what it means to accept responsibility for one's actions.

Right now, our society as a whole is extremely concerned that someone is going to take advantage of them. They fear one-upmanship. The motto seems to be: "Strike the other person before the other person strikes you." By teaching responsibility, we can change our thinking to accommodate compromise and working things out, and move to forgive and ask forgiveness.

Another part of teaching responsibility is something we already see happening in some states: the sponsoring of parenting classes that teach parents how to go through the divorce process while keeping their children as emotionally intact as possible. Such courses would necessarily include issues surrounding child support.

There is good news about this model for the future: Many of these twelve elements are already springing up in various places across the U.S. But true success will be to see them as a routine part of child-support procedure in all fifty states.

THE TRUE IDEAL

The highest goal at which we as a country can aim is keeping our families intact. Across the United States, people are recognizing the value of this goal. Even politicians, both Republicans and Democrats, are speaking out about the need to preserve and support the family.

If we want to have intact families in the U.S., attorneys and the public at large are going to have to look at things differently. As attorneys who work with struggling families every day, we join the growing ranks of judges and lawyers who are crying out for reconciliation in marriages and for better premarital counseling to start couples out on the right foot. Our families and our country cannot continue along the destructive route we are currently taking.

Until we see improvements in the future, the burden of responsibility for your child's support rests on your shoulders. Educate yourself about the way the child-support system works in our country as well as in the state where you live. Understand just what support involves. Do your homework and walk wisely and maturely through the process ahead of you. Be aware of both your rights and the hurdles you will be likely to encounter along your way to reaching them.

Don't be thrown by the emotional impact that is sure to assail you—and likely already has—instead, refuse to allow it to overwhelm you. Take every opportunity to be encouraged by reminding yourself that by enforcing the child-support laws you are caring for your child. And later on, when you are safely through the process, be willing to work for improvements that will make it easier for the families who come along after you.

Your child is well worth the effort. Every child is.

▼ ▼

Information Resources

Child Support Technology Transfer Project
5530 Wisconsin Avenue, Suite 1600
Chevy Chase, MD 20815

National Child Support Enforcement Association
Hall of Statutes
400 North Capitol Street, Suite 372
Washington, DC 20001-1512

The federal government offers a free question and answer guide entitled *Handbook on Child Support Enforcement*. To receive a copy write:
U.S. Department of Health and Human Services
Office of Child Support Enforcement
PII-4th Floor, 901 D Street SW
Washington, DC 20047

The Association for Children for Enforcement of Support (ACES) is a self-help group with 300 chapters in forty-nine states. They provide answers to questions about state agencies and let you know how to use them to get what you need. ACES claims a 75 percent success rate in helping people collect child support money, and their services are free. For more information or a free packet write:

ACES
2260 Upton Avenue
Toledo, OH 43606
(800)537-7072

For information on mediation services contact:
Academy of Family Mediators
P.O. Box 10501
Eugene, OR 97440

American Arbitration Association
201 East Pine Street, Suite 800
Orlando, FL 32801
(407)648-1185

Family Advocate
P.O. Box 295
Westport, CT 06881

National Institute for Dispute Resolution
1726 M Street NW, Suite 500
Washington, DC 20036
(202)466-4764

Society of Professionals in Dispute Resolution (SPIDR)
815 - 15th Street NW, Suite 530
Washington, DC 20005
(202)986-1118

▼ ▼

Sample Worksheets

FINANCIAL AFFIDAVIT AND CHILD-SUPPORT GUIDELINES WORKSHEET

Family Division, Case No. _____

State of _____

County of _____

Before me, this day personally appeared _____,
Husband/Wife, who being duly sworn, deposes and says that
the following information is true and correct according to
his/her best knowledge and belief:

EMPLOYMENT AND INCOME

Occupation: _____

Employed by: _____

Employer's address: _____

Social security number: _____

Pay period: Weekly ❑ Bi-Weekly ❑ Twice Monthly ❑ Monthly ❑

Average gross monthly income: (1 month equals 4.3 weeks)

Regular salary or wages: $ _____

Bonuses, commissions, allowances, overtime, tips,
and similar payments: $ _____

Business income from sources such as self-employment,
partnership, close corporations and/or independent contracts
(gross receipts minus ordinary and necessary expenses
required to produce income): $ _____

Disability benefits: $ _____

Worker's compensation: $ _____

Unemployment compensation: $ _____

Pension, retirements, or annuity payments: $ _____

Social security benefits: $ _____

Spousal support received from previous marriage: $ _____

Interest and dividends: $ _____

Rental income (gross receipts minus ordinary and
necessary expenses required to produce income): $ _____

Income from royalties, trust, or estates: $ _____

Reimbursed expenses and in kind payments to the extent
that they reduce personal living expenses: $ _____

Gains derived from dealing in property
(not including non-recurring gains): $ _____

Itemize any other income of recurring nature: $ _____

TOTAL MONTHLY INCOME $ _____

AVERAGE MONTHLY EXPENSES

Household

Mortgage or rent payments	$ _____
Property taxes and ins.	$ _____
Electricity	$ _____
Water, garbage, and sewer	$ _____
Telephone	$ _____
Fuel, oil or natural gas	$ _____
Repairs and maintenance	$ _____
Lawn and pool care	$ _____
Pest control	$ _____
Housewares	$ _____
Food and grocery items	$ _____
Meals outside home	$ _____
Other	$ _____

Automobile

Gasoline and oil	$ _____
Repairs	$ _____
Auto tag and license	$ _____
Insurance	$ _____
Other	$ _____

Children's Expenses

Child care and babysitters	$ _____
School tuition	$ _____
School supplies	$ _____
Lunch money	$ _____
Allowance	$ _____
Clothing	$ _____
Medical, dental, prescriptions	$ _____
Vitamins	$ _____
Barber/beauty parlor	$ _____
Cosmetics/toiletries	$ _____
Gifts for special holidays	$ _____
Other	$ _____

Payments to Creditors

_____	$ _____
_____	$ _____
_____	$ _____
_____	$ _____
_____	$ _____
_____	$ _____

Insurance

Health	$ _____
Life and disability	$ _____
Other	$ _____

Other Expenses Not Listed Above

PERSONAL EXPENSES

Dry cleaning and laundry	$ _____
Clothing	$ _____
Medical/dental/ prescriptions	$ _____
Beauty parlor/barber	$ _____
Cosmetics/toiletries	$ _____
Gifts (special holidays)	$ _____

PETS

Grooming	$ _____
Veterinarian	$ _____

MEMBERSHIP DUES

Professional dues	$ _____
Social dues	$ _____

OTHER EXPENSES

Entertainment	$ _____
Vacations	$ _____
Publications	$ _____
Church and charities	$ _____
Miscellaneous	$ _____
Other	
_____	$ _____
_____	$ _____
_____	$ _____
_____	$ _____

TOTAL MONTHLY EXPENSES	$ _____
NET OR DEFICIT	$ _____

Less Deductions

Federal, state and local income taxes (corrected for filing status and actual number of withholding allowances)	$ _____
FICA or self-employment tax (annualized)	$ _____
Mandatory union dues	$ _____
Mandatory retirement	$ _____
Health ins. payments	$ _____
Court ordered child-support payments actually paid	$ _____
TOTAL DEDUCTIONS	$ _____
TOTAL NET MONTHLY INCOME	$ _____

CHILD SUPPORT GUIDELINES WORKSHEET
(MONTHLY SUPPORT)

I. A. Husband's Total Net Income $ _____ per week (x) 4.3 = $ _____
    B. Wife's Total Net Income $ _____ per week (x) 4.3 = $ _____

II. Custodial Parent's Percentage of Combined Income:

_____ - _____ = _____ %
Noncustodial Parent's Net Income   Combined Net Income

III. A. Guidelines of Recommended Child Support: $ _____
     B. Day-care Costs (per F.S. 61.30[7]) $ _____
     C. Total: $ _____

Husband's Responsibility toward support _____ % of $ _____ = $ _____
Wife's Responsibility toward support _____ % of $ _____ = $ _____

TOTAL $ _____

ASSETS AND LIABILITIES

(Allocate between husband and wife based upon present title ownership.
If joint, allocate equally.)

Assets

DESCRIPTION	VALUE	HUSBAND	WIFE
Cash:			
Stocks:			
Bonds:			
Notes:			
Real property:			
Automobiles:			
Contents of home:			
Contents of apt.:			
Jewelry:			
Life insurance (cash surrender value):			
Other assets:			
TOTAL ASSETS	$ _____	$ _____	$ _____

Liabilities

CREDITOR	SECURITY	BALANCE	HUSBAND	WIFE
_____	_____	_____	_____	_____
_____	_____	_____	_____	_____
_____	_____	_____	_____	_____
_____	_____	_____	_____	_____
_____	_____	_____	_____	_____
TOTAL LIABILITIES		$ _____	$ _____	$ _____
NET WORTH *(TOTAL ASSETS LESS TOTAL LIABILITIES)*		$ _____	$ _____	$ _____

_____ *AFFIANT*

SWORN TO AND SUBSCRIBED before me this   day of   , 19   .

_____ *NOTARY PUBLIC*

▼ ▼

Family Law Enforcement in the Fifty States (As of 1994)

ENFORCEMENT OF CHILD-SUPPORT ORDERS

	States with specific support long-arm statutes	States with authority to have payment made directly to court officer	States that allow wage assignments income deductions
Alabama	X	X	X
Alaska	X	X	X
Arizona		X	X
Arkansas			X
California		X	X
Colorado		X	X
Connecticut		X	X
Delaware	X	X	X
District of Columbia	X	X	X
Florida	X	X	X
Georgia	X	X	X
Hawaii			X
Idaho		X	X
Illinois	X	X	X
Indiana	X	X	X
Iowa			X
Kansas	X	X	X
Kentucky	X		
Louisianna			
Maine	X		X
Maryland			
Massachusetts	X	X	X
Michigan	X	X	X
Minnesota		X	X
Mississippi	X		
Missouri	X	X	X

	States with specific support long-arm statutes	States with authority to have payment made directly to court officer	States that allow wage assignments income deductions
Montana			x
Nebraska			
Nevada			
New Hampshire		x	x
New Jersey			
New Mexico			x
New York	x	x	x
North Carolina	x	x	x
North Dakota		x	x
Ohio	x	x	x
Oklahoma	x	x	x
Oregon			x
Pennsylvania		x	x
Rhode Island			x
South Carolina	x	x	x
South Dakota	x	x	x
Texas			x
Tennessee	x	x	x
Utah	x	x	x
Vermont			x
Virginia	x	x	x
Washington	x	x	x
West Virginia			
Wisconsin	x	x	x
Wyoming			x

▼ ▼

Glossary

ABSENT PARENT: A person who is absent from the home and is legally responsible for providing financial support for a dependent child.

ACKNOWLEDGED FATHER: The natural father of a child born out of wedlock for whom PATERNITY has been established.

ACTION: An ordinary proceeding in a court in which one person prosecutes another.

AGREEMENT: A transcribed or written resolution of the disputed issues when the parties have resolved issues in the case.

AID TO FAMILIES WITH DEPENDENT CHILDREN (AFDC): Government financial aid given for the support of children whose parent or parents are not living in the home.

ALIMONY: Money paid to a person by his or her ex-spouse for that person's support.

ALLEGATION: The assertion of a person made in pleading a case, setting out what is expected to be proven.

ALLEGED FATHER: A person who has been named as the father of a child born out of wedlock, but for whom PATERNITY has not been established.

APPEAL: A person's request to a higher court to review the ruling made in a lower court for possible errors that would justify overruling the lower court's JUDGMENT and perhaps grant a new trial.

APPLICANT: The CARETAKER relative, the children, and anyone else whose needs are considered in determining the amount of assistance.

ARREARAGE: Unpaid support money owed by a responsible person.

BURDEN OF PROOF: The duty of proving a fact on an issue raised between two people.

CARETAKER: The person responsible for a child's health or welfare who has temporary or legal custody of a dependent child.

CHILD SUPPORT: Support for a child. This is not taxable to the recipient nor deductible to the payer.

COMPLAINT: The formal written document filed in a court in which the person initiating the ACTION sets forth the names of the parties, the ALLEGATION, and the goal of the action.

COMPLAINANT: A person who seeks to initiate court proceedings against another person.

CONTEMPT OF COURT: The willful failure to comply with a court ORDER, JUDGMENT, or decree by a party to the ACTION, which may be punishable in a variety of ways.

CUSTODIAL PARENT: The parent who has actual custody of a child.

DEFENDANT: In civil proceedings, the person responding to the COMPLAINT. In criminal proceedings, the accused.

EMANCIPATION: The point at which a child may be treated as an adult and in some states when the duty of support terminates.

FEDERAL PARENT LOCATOR SERVICE (FPLS): The system devised and operated by OCSE for the purpose of searching federal government records to locate ABSENT PARENTS.

GARNISHMENT: Money withheld directly from someone's paycheck to pay a debt, such as unpaid CHILD SUPPORT, based on court ORDER.

GUARDIAN AD LITEM (GAL): A layperson or lawyer appointed by the court to represent the children.

GUIDELINES: A recommended amount of CHILD SUPPORT based on a formula, usually established by state STATUTE.

HEARING: Any proceeding before the court for the purpose of resolving disputed issues through the presentation of testimony, offers of proof, and argument.

HEARING OFFICER: A person appointed by the court—a non-judicial officer—to hear the facts of a case and give a report to that court with appropriate recommendations for a ruling.

IMPUTED INCOME: All available moneys paid by a corporation for the benefit of its employee or shareholder, or income assumed by the court because a person has voluntarily reduced his or her income.

INCOME DEDUCTION: Income automatically withheld by the employer from a paycheck for the payment of CHILD SUPPORT or other obligations, based on court ORDER.

JUDGMENT: The official decision of a court on the respective rights of the parties involved in an ACTION.

LIEN: An encumbrance placed against someone's property or asset as a result of a financial obligation owed by the owner of the property.

MEDIATION: A process that provides for the intervention of an acceptable, impartial third-party who helps the two parents reach a mutually acceptable settlement of their differences. Since at this time mediation is purely voluntary, either parent can reject further participation at any time.

MOTION TO MODIFY: A formal request to the court to change a prior ORDER regarding custody, CHILD SUPPORT, ALIMONY, or any other ORDER from the court.

NET INCOME: Gross income minus allowable deductions.

NONCUSTODIAL PARENT: The parent with whom a child does not permanently reside, who does not have actual custody of the child.

OFFICE OF CHILD SUPPORT ENFORCEMENT (OCSE): The government division that searches federal government records to locate ABSENT PARENTS. See FEDERAL PARENT LOCATOR SERVICE.

ORDER: The court's ruling on a motion requiring the parties to do certain things or setting forth their rights and responsibilities. An order is generally written, signed by the judge, and filed with the court.

PATERNITY: The establishment of paternal status (the father's identity), including rights and responsibilities.

PATERNITY CASE: An ACTION to determine the parentage of a child born out of wedlock.

PAYOR: An individual required to transfer money to someone else for CHILD SUPPORT, ALIMONY, or other obligations.

PAYEE: The person receiving payment for CHILD SUPPORT, ALIMONY, or other obligations.

PUTATIVE FATHER: A person who has been named as the father of a child born out of wedlock but for whom PATERNITY has not been established. See also ALLEGED FATHER.

QUALIFIED MEDICAL CHILD SUPPORT ORDER (QMCSO): An order requiring an employer to withhold health insurance premiums from the noncustodial parent's paycheck.

REAL PROPERTY: Land-related property.

REBUTTABLE PRESUMPTION: A legal assumption of truth that can be refuted by the presentation of additional and extraordinary facts.

RESPONSIBLE PARENT: Any person who is legally responsible to provide financial support for a dependent child.

REVISED UNIFORM RECIPROCAL ENFORCEMENT OF SUPPORT ACT (RURESA): An update of the UNIFORM RECIPROCAL ENFORCEMENT SUPPORT ACT (URESA).

SEIZURE: The taking of an object from the person who possesses it by a law enforcement officer.

SHARED PARENTING AGREEMENT: A written agreement entered into by both parents, detailing that the parents will share in the decision making with regard to the raising of their child.

SPOUSAL SUPPORT: Money paid to a person by his or her ex-spouse for that person's support. Same as ALIMONY.

STATE PARENT LOCATOR SERVICE (SPLS): The organization in a state charged with the duty of locating an ABSENT PARENT for establishing or enforcing CHILD-SUPPORT obligations.

STATUTES: Laws enacted by legislatures.

SUBPOENA: A document served on a party or witness requiring appearance in court. Failure to comply with a subpoena could result in punishment by the court.

SUBSTANTIVE LAW: Law that governs the rights, duties, and liabilities of the people and defines the issues that the evidence must prove.

SUMMONS: A notice to a DEFENDANT that an ACTION against him or her has been started in court. If the defendant fails to answer within a specified time, a JUDGMENT will be taken against him or her.

TERM DECREASING LIFE INSURANCE: A life insurance policy obtained to secure payment of CHILD SUPPORT, decreasing in amount each month as payments are made.

TITLE IV-D: Refers to Title IV-D of the Social Security Act. The federal statute that provides for enforcement of child support to be undertaken with government funds.

UNIFORM INTERSTATE FAMILY SUPPORT ACT (UIFSA): A law similar to URESA in which support is enforced between states but only one court maintains continuing jurisdiction.

UNIFORM RECIPROCAL ENFORCEMENT SUPPORT ACT (URESA): A uniform law that sets forth reciprocal legislation concerning the enforcement of support between the states. All fifty states have passed a form of URESA.

WAGE ASSIGNMENT: The deduction of child-support ARREARAGE by an employer from wages (or salary). See also INCOME DEDUCTION.

Authors

NANCY S. PALMER received her B.A. in 1974 (magna cum laude) and her M.A. (summa cum laude) in 1976 from the University of Central Florida. Ms. Palmer is a former member of the Executive Council of the Family Law Section of the Florida Bar, the former chairman of the Section's Mediation, Legislation, and Child Support Committees, and also served as chairman of the Section in 1993–1994. She is the former chairman of the Florida Bar Committee on the Legal Needs of Children (1986–1988).

Ms. Palmer is a Florida board certified marital and family lawyer and was rated AV by Martindale Hubble after eight years of practice. She also assisted in drafting the first shared parenting pamphlet published by the Florida Bar. She is past chairman of the Family Law Section of the Academy of Florida Trial Lawyers.

Ms. Palmer was recognized by the Florida Supreme Court and the Alternative Dispute Resolution Center in September 1992 for her work in family mediation. She trains mediators under the Florida Supreme Court's Family Mediation Certification standards forty-hour course as a primary trainer with materials she developed. She was also chosen for the state's initial family mediation training team in 1988. She has been a trained family mediator since 1984 and has also trained guardians *ad litem* throughout the state on behalf of the State of Florida Guardian Ad Litem Program.

Ms. Palmer has expertise in adoption and was selected for admission into the National Academy of Adoption Attorneys in 1991. She served as the general master in *Mize v. Mize* and has argued numerous amicus briefs on family law and children's issues in front of Florida's highest court.

Ms. Palmer has received many state and national honors including being chosen as one of America's ten most Outstanding Young Women of 1988. In 1993, she was honored by the Florida Supreme Court with the Tobias Simon Award for her pro bono legal services to the poor and unrepresented.

Ms. Palmer is currently a shareholder in the office of Nancy S. Palmer, P.A., and practices only mediation because of her strong belief in the process. Some of Ms. Palmer's publications are available upon request. Currently, she serves as co-chairman of the Alternative Dispute Resolution Committee of the Family Law Section of the American Bar Association.

ANA TANGEL-RODRIGUEZ represents the State of Florida, Department of Revenue in Orlando, Florida. Her law firm, Tangel-Rodriguez & Associates, is devoted solely to the enforcement of child support.

Ana received her B.A. with honors in English education from the University of Central Florida in 1975. She received her Juris Doctor in 1977 from the Florida State University College of Law.

From 1979 to 1981 Ana was an assistant state attorney handling misdemeanor and felony jury trials, juvenile proceedings, and prosecution of capital offenses.

She was also an assistant professor at the University of Central Florida, teaching upper level courses in family law, civil litigation, and legal research and writing.

Since 1985 Ana's practice has been exclusively dedicated to child-support litigation. In addition she has presented a workshop at the Florida Family Support Council Conference, training seminars for local child-support enforcement case analysts, and provided input on upcoming legislation. She has appeared on *In Focus*, a public affairs television program, discussing the Child Support Enforcement Program, and has lectured at the Orange County Bar Legal Aid Society's Domestic Relations Seminar on legal updates in child-support enforcement. Additionally she co-authored a published article entitled *The Department and You: A Guide to Child Support Enforcement*.

In 1983 Ana was presented with an award by the Orange County Legal Aid Society in recognition and appreciation of her work in the area of family law.

In 1994 her law firm received the Orange County Bar Legal Aid Society's Award for Excellence for pro bono representation of the poor.

Ana has been a member of numerous civic and professional associations. She has been a director on the boards of Spouse Abuse, Women's Resource Center, and the Central Florida Association of Women Lawyers. She is also a member of the Family Law Committee of both the Florida Bar and Orange County Bar Association. Ana has recently been appointed by the chief justice of the Florida supreme court to the state's Mediator Qualifications Board.

Ana lives in Orlando, Florida, with her husband, Jose Rodriquez, a circuit court judge in the Ninth Judicial Circuit and her two children, Ani and Michael.